HEARTBEATS IN THE MUCK

BOOKS BY JOHN WALDMAN

*Sturgeon Biodiversity and
Conservation* (co-editor)

*Hempstead Harbor: History, Ecology, and
Environmental Challenges* (co-editor)

Stripers: An Angler's Anthology (editor)

Heartbeats in the Muck

HEARTBEATS
IN THE MUCK

THE HISTORY, SEA LIFE,
AND ENVIRONMENT
OF NEW YORK HARBOR

JOHN WALDMAN

THE LYONS PRESS

For my father,
who introduced me to the shore,
and my mother,
who encouraged me to explore it.

Design by Cindy LaBreacht

Printed in the United States of America

10 9 8 7 6 5 4 3 2 1

Library of Congress Cataloging-in-Publication Data
Waldman, John R.
    Heartbeats in the muck: the history, sea life, and environment of New York Harbor / John Waldman.
        p.   cm.
    Includes bibliographical references.
    ISBN 1-55821-720-7 (hc)
    1. Estuarine biology—New York Harbor (N.Y. and N.J.)
2. Estuarine ecology—New York Harbor (N.Y. and N.J.) 3. New York Harbor (N.Y. and N.J.). I. Title.
QH105.N7W35   1999
577.7'86346—dc21   99-36292
                                                            CIP

"Man marks the earth with ruin, his control stops with the shore."

> George Gordon, Lord Byron
> "Apostrophe to the Ocean" (1818)

———————

"The bulk of the water in New York Harbor is oily, dirty, and germy. Men on the mud suckers, the big harbor dredges, say you could bottle it and sell it for poison."

> Joseph Mitchell
> "The Bottom of the Harbor"
> *The New Yorker* (1951)

"The efficiency and pragmatism of the cutting and removal within waters and whirlpools overwhelms."

> John Hejduk
> The Printed Whale (In Search of)
> in *The New York Waterfront* (1997)

ACKNOWLEDGMENTS

I AM GRATEFUL TO the many New York Harbor aficionados who helped me prepare this book. Visits to its various corners were led or hosted by Janet Duffy-Anderson, Len Houston, Ron Ingold, Paul Kerlinger, Ben Longstreth, Dave Secor, Joe Shastay, Bill Sheehan, John Young, and the Brooklyn Center for the Urban Environment. Useful information, images, or both were provided by Abu Moulta Ali, Helena Andreyko, Adam Brown, Norman Brouwer, James Carlton, Curtis Cravens, C. Braxton Dew, Cathy Drew, Owen Foote, Rob Gill, Ben Longstreth, Rob Maass, Clyde MacKenzie, Virginia Rolston Parrott, Don Riepe, Dave Taft, Charles Traub, and John Young. Portions or all of the manuscript were reviewed by Helena Andreyko, Henry Bokuniewicz, Art Glowka, Clay Hiles, Paul Kerlinger, Tom Lake, Ben Longstreth, Molly Rauch, Michael Rivlin, Nancy Steinberg, Dennis Suszkowski, Carol Waldman, Isaac Wirgin, and William Zeisel. Special thanks to Michael Rivlin for suggesting that what was envisioned as a magazine article should instead grow into a book, and to Nick Lyons and Anja Schmidt of the Lyons Press for agreeing. Finally, my deepest appreciation to Carol, Laura, and Steve for their steadfast support and for leaving time for me to work on those many evenings and weekends.

CONTENTS

Introduction / 13

1

The Essential Harbor / 19

2

Vita Marinae / 31

3

The Medium: Sewers, Sludge, and
Other Forms of Water Torture / 81

4

The Vessel: Bank and Bottom,
Bulldozers and Blasts / 115

5

How Is the Harbor Doing? / 157

Bibliography / 167
Index / 171

INTRODUCTION

NEW YORKERS HAVE a dark fascination with their surrounding waters. Where else is it expected that sometime during mid-April, as the depths warm, bacterial activity will bloat the previous winter's bounty of murders and suicides and cause them to rise to the harbor's surface—a synchronized resurrection of the damned that captains call "Floaters' Week." New York Harbor is a place so mysterious that things go bump in the night in the daytime, too. The public's cognizance of its ecological health leans more toward this black view—a harbor of utter lifelessness or a chemical stew featuring gasping flounder—than the present reality of a simultaneously stressed but thriving ecosystem.

No one has rendered this bleak perspective better than Saul Steinberg in his frontispiece to Joseph Mitchell's classic, *The Bottom of the Harbor*. In his simple sketch Manhattan appears above the waterline as a bundle of gloriously towering spires, the image's visual weight balanced offshore by Lady Liberty. Commerce is represented by a tugboat towing a cruise ship. Below the surface the composition is spare, with natural life embodied by only two passing fish. But the scene is made memorable by a critical addition—the mystique and dark romance of the harbor are symbolized by a human skeleton tumbling out of a fifty-five-gallon drum.

Growing up in New York City in the 1960s and traveling to cleaner shores to fish and swim, I shared the general naive disdain of the harbor environment and could scarcely believe rumors of fine angling beneath raw sewage. Riding highways along the East River or Upper New York Bay, I wondered what creatures, if any, lurked under the floating garbage and oil slicks and among the rotting pilings. But even in its most ravaged state those few brave enough to buck preconceptions or sufficiently intimate with it by virtue of their station in life or some accident of geography could see, and at times enjoy, the swirling milieu of nature still served up by the choking harbor.

Also in that decade the nation's environmental movement began, to a large extent, not far north of New York Harbor—in the Highlands of the Hudson River. It was there that author Carl Carmer and other concerned citizens organized to fight the building of new, and the operating practices of old, electric-generating plants, in the process spawning influential environmental advocacy groups such as Clearwater, Scenic Hudson, and the Hudson River Fishermen's Association. These organizations, along with their national counterparts, played pivotal roles in the passage of laws that were novel for their time and in the enforcement of long-forgotten but environmentally astute statutes, which together started to stem New York Harbor's decline. And a landmark agreement among environmentalists, regulators, and the electric utilities over the complex suite of Hudson River power-plant issues resulted in the creation of a unique entity entirely focused on the Hudson River and New York Harbor—the Hudson River Foundation for Science and Environmental Research.

Later, while a graduate student at the City University of New York and the American Museum of Natural History in the 1980s, I worked for one winter as a field biologist on the most contentious environmental issue ever to crash the shores of Manhattan—the ecological consequences of the proposed West Side Highway Project, called Westway. The Westway issue arrived at a time when knowledge of the condition of the harbor's life lagged behind the actual gains that were being made through the cleansing of its waters. Although the scientific outcome of the final Westway study was inconclusive, the study did reveal a dynamic and flourishing fish life that helped sway perceptions of Manhattan's coastline from the home of a few curious and unusually hardy invertebrate and piscine relicts to an important element of the regional ecosystem.

Fortunately for me, on the day after my employment on the Westway study ended and I sat at my kitchen table reviewing the want ads, my telephone rang; I was invited to interview for a scientific position with the Hudson River Foundation. I got the job and for more than a decade have been immersed in the never-ending environmental conundrums, wildly diverse personae, ever-mutating governmental programs, and enormous potential of New York Harbor.

New York Harbor is singular—at once familiar, taken for granted, dismissed, and exotic; and ironically it is distant in its nearness to the extent that it's been aptly described as an "urban wilderness." But with so many people living along its shores, with dozens of colleges and universities within easy reach, and with a far-from-secret litany of problems imploring attention, why hasn't knowledge of New York Harbor accumulated in proportion to its population and proximity?

15

For the two centuries prior to 1900 American biologists, including local naturalists, were mainly engaged in discovering and classifying the continent's plants and animals, largely in a westward direction. Meanwhile, an increasing populace and expanding industry despoiled the harbor, the deterioration eliciting not study of its natural ecology but examination by engineers of its pollution problems. And because it took so long for the will and means to begin to reverse the flow and accumulation of hundreds of years of contamination, the harbor remained distinctly off-putting to researchers. Why study your own filthy and seemingly mundane backyard when whales and coral reefs, the Red Sea, the Hawaiian Islands, and the Antarctic Ocean beckon?

What has been learned about life's workings in New York Harbor has come from diverse and peculiar sources: the rare parochially intrigued scientist, obsessed and dedicated amateurs, professional divers sent down by industry or their own curiosity, serendipitous surveys performed for environmental impact statements preceding construction projects, and government programs that bloom and then fade, adding some bytes to the knowledge base before the next program follows.

The collective insight from the rediscovery of a harbor reborn can be viewed from many directions. I believe the essence of its story is the creatures themselves and their survival in the face of the two grand insults that urban humanity has imposed on this estuary: degradation of the medium, the waters, and disfigurement of the vessel that cradles those waters—bank and bottom, the habitat of the harbor.

This book is an environmental tour through New York Harbor in space and time as seen through the eyes of someone seduced by its jaunty resilience in the face of those insults.

HEARTBEATS IN THE MUCK

1

THE ESSENTIAL HARBOR

"I do not know much about gods;
but I think that the river

Is a strong brown god—sullen,
untamed and intractable."

T. S. Eliot
"The Dry Salvages" (1943)

1

NEW YORK HARBOR HAS BEEN inconsistently defined, existing as much as an abstraction as a geographic entity. I prefer to view it broadly as a sprawling estuarine complex, recognizing the interconnectedness of its many drainages. And if estuaries are places where fresh water blends with seawater, then New York Harbor is a festival of estuaries, an illustrated hierarchical array.

The heart of the harbor is the Upper and Lower New York Bays: auricle and ventricle. The Upper Bay receives the runoff of much of New York State via the Hudson River, saline in summer almost to Poughkeepsie and tidal at all times to Troy. I have stood on Troy's shore, nearly 150 miles inland from the coast, and

Where the Hudson and East Rivers meet at lower Manhattan. (Charles H. Traub)

watched the push of the sea raise the water level inches in just minutes. The Hudson River begins officially in Lake Tear of the Clouds, high on Mount Marcy in the Adirondacks, but the river really starts in an infinite number of places—anywhere droplets gather in the Hudson Valley. Native Americans referred to the Hudson as *Muhheakunnuk*, loosely translated as "the river that flows both ways." (It was also known as *Cahotateda*, "river from beyond the peaks.") Waters originating from Catskill Mountain bogs, dairy farms of the Mohawk River Valley, little corners of Connecticut, Vermont, and Massachusetts, and urban tributaries in river towns such as Beacon and Newburgh mix in the Hudson, where for weeks they may travel incrementally southward while retreating slightly on every incoming tide, only to flow straight to sea through the Verrazano Narrows, or to whip around the Battery at the foot of Manhattan to be sent at five knots to Long Island Sound through the articular tidal strait of the East River. Likewise, the mini estuaries of the Hackensack and Passaic Rivers slowly

View of the Upper Bay toward Verrazano Narrows Bridge. (Charles H. Traub)

press Newark Bay waters through two Dutch-named capillaries: the Kill Van Kull and the Arthur Kill.

The Lower Bay connects the flow from the Upper Bay with the near-ocean waters of the New York Bight, the triangle of submerged shelf and canyon running from Montauk, New York, to Cape May, New Jersey. Backing into the Lower Bay are more modest estuaries, the Raritan and the combined output of the Shrewsbury and Navesink Rivers. Completing the complex are other large waterways flushed with copious quantities of seawater, including Rockaway Inlet and Jamaica Bay, and quiescent dead ends that have accumulated fabled amounts of corruption, such as Newtown Creek, the Gowanus Canal, and Flushing Bay, which flushes poorly.

Punctuating this watery network are islands, almost three dozen if those near the Long Island Sound end of the East River are included. Most are natural; some are not. Many are small and unoccupied; a few are large and host unique populaces. Roosevelt

Island is home to hundreds of thousands of residents who savor the isolation and small-town quality their sliver of land between Manhattan and Queens offers; Governors Island houses a skeletal Coast Guard staff; Rikers Island's incarcerated would prefer to be "off island"; and Hart Island sequesters the city's indigent dead in its potter's field. A few of the harbor's islands prop ruins, such as the crumbling quarantine buildings on the East River's North Brother Island that once hosted Typhoid Mary. And East High Meadow, South Brother, Shooters, and other islands are essential nesting and feeding grounds for the celebrated bird colonies of New York Harbor.

2

New York Harbor has sustained such wrenching changes in just four centuries since Europeans arrived that it is convenient to imagine the harbor prior to then as existing in idyllic stability. But in fact New York Harbor is a very recent phenomenon and the product of complex and titanic forces.

Much of the present topography of New York Harbor was sculpted during the Pleistocene, or Ice Age, which included broad glacial advances and retreats. New York City was the southern limit of an ice sheet that covered much of northern North America with up to two miles of frozen water; even in the Upper New York Bay the glacier was about three hundred feet thick—the height of many of the office buildings that ring it today. This unfathomable force moved southward to the harbor's latitude at least twice, leveling the land and carrying massive amounts of gravel and boulders, which were left behind as the glacier retreated. Indeed, the advancing and receding ice sheet left the deepest deposits of material at its very edge; these terminal moraines form the backbones of Long Island (including Queens and Brooklyn) and Staten Island. When you stand on the north shore of Queens, you are really standing on mineral scrapings from upstate New York and New England. The wide low-elevation areas along the south shore of Long Island, including Brooklyn and Queens, and Staten Island are nothing more than the finer-grained sediments that washed out from the hilly moraines.

During peak glacial advances the sea level was four hundred feet lower than at present, and the Hudson River flowed another 120 miles across the coastal plain, gouging the Hudson Canyon. It also did not follow the bed it occupies today. Gaps in the ridges of the Palisades and Watchung Mountains carved well before the Ice Age suggest that the Hudson crossed the Palisades near Sparkill, a little north of the harbor, then flowed southwest across the Watchungs near Paterson, New Jersey, and then to the ocean through the channel of the present Raritan River. Also, Mr. Sidney Horenstein, a geologist with the American Museum of Natural History, presents a convincing case for the Hudson River having at one time coursed through Flushing Meadow Park, the east bank near the present Van Wyck Expressway extension, the west bank where the Grand Central Parkway lies, before the river discharged to the ocean through Jamaica Bay.

Today the flow from the Upper Bay punches to the Lower Bay through the Verrazano Narrows, an outlet created almost yester-day in geological time. About six thousand years ago the final advance of the Wisconsin glacier deposited a moraine across the harbor between Brooklyn and Staten Island. Meltwater from the receding glacier then breached this moraine, carving the narrows, an earth-shaping event perhaps witnessed by Native Americans. The retreat of the Wisconsin glacier also left large collections of

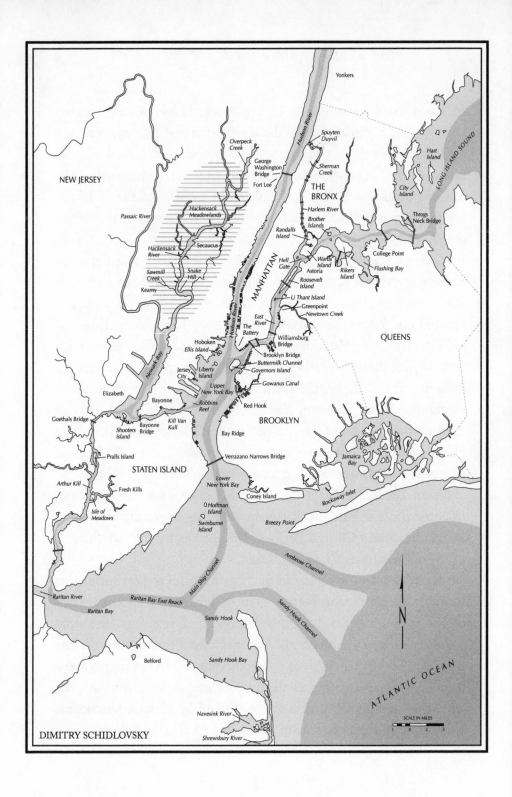

Yonkers

NEW JERSEY

Overpeck
Creek

Spuyten
Duyvil

George
Washington
Bridge

Fort Lee

Sherman
Creek

Hart
Island

City
Island

THE
BRONX

Passaic River

Hackensack
Meadowlands

Harlem River

Throgs
Neck Bridge

Hackensack
River

Secaucus

Brother
Islands

Randalls
Island

LONG ISLAND SOUND

Sawmill
Creek

Snake
Hill

Wards
Island

College Point

Kearny

Hell
Gate

Astoria

Roosevelt
Island

Rikers
Island

Flushing Bay

MANHATTAN

U Thant Island

Greenpoint

Newtown Creek

QUEENS

East
River

The
Battery

Hoboken

Ellis Island

Williamsburg
Bridge

Brooklyn Bridge

Buttermilk Channel

Jersey
City

Liberty
Island

Governors Island

Gowanus Canal

Upper
New York Bay

Robbins
Reef

Red Hook

Elizabeth

Bayonne

BROOKLYN

Newark Bay

Goethals Bridge

Shooters
Island

Bayonne
Bridge

Kill Van
Kull

Bay Ridge

Pralls Island

Verrazano Narrows Bridge

Arthur Kill

STATEN ISLAND

Lower
New York Bay

Jamaica
Bay

Fresh Kills

Coney Island

Rockaway Inlet

Isle of
Meadows

Hoffman
Island

Swinburne
Island

Breezy Point

Ambrose Channel

Raritan River

Main Ship Channel

Raritan Bay East Reach

Sandy Hook Channel

Raritan Bay

Sandy Hook

Belford

Sandy Hook Bay

ATLANTIC OCEAN

N

SCALE IN MILES
1   0   1   2   3

Navesink River

Shrewsbury River

DIMITRY SCHIDLOVSKY

meltwater known as Lake Flushing, Lake Hackensack, and, farther inland, Lake Passaic. Clay settled out in Lake Hackensack for some three thousand years, after which it slowly drained and the sea level rose, sending tidewater inland and creating the Hackensack Meadowlands.

The lower Hudson is a fjord and as such is more an arm of the sea than a river. The four-hundred- to six-hundred-foot cliffs of the Palisades, perhaps the most dramatic geological feature of the harbor portion of the Hudson, are diabase—six-sided pillars of black rock jelled from molten lava injected sideways between layers of long since eroded-away sandstone. The bedrock of Manhattan is Fordham schist, Inwood marble, and gneiss of the White Mountain series, the same range that underlies Philadelphia, Baltimore, and Washington, D.C. Hidden six hundred feet under the harbor lies an important geological marker—Camerons Line, a forty- to sixty-yard-wide band of crushed rock believed to be the ancient point of contact between North America and a portion of land grafted to the continent.

Although the harbor's bottom is lined with almost every conceivable class of sediment, from fine red clay to boulders, much of it is of a flocculent material that looks like black mayonnaise. Fine gas bubbles from decomposing detritus infuse the muds, which are devoid of oxygen not far below their surface. Some of the sediment deposits are deep—three hundred feet of material lies above the bedrock where the Holland and Lincoln Tunnels cross below the Hudson River, and more than seven hundred feet farther upriver. The salt marshes of the harbor are only about four thousand years old, having had to wait to begin their formation for the postglacial climate to warm and for silt to accumulate in quiet backwaters.

New York Harbor's fifteen hundred square miles are washed by what are some of the most complicated tides anywhere, and water circulates in all directions. On the flood some 260 billion cubic feet of water pass through the Verrazano Narrows and upriver between Manhattan and New Jersey. But the Coriolis force (from the earth's rotation) nudges salt water farther upstream along the east bank of the lower Hudson River than on the western shore. The Hudson, like many estuaries, stratifies to a degree, the lighter freshwater outflow riding above denser salt water moving upriver from the ocean, called the underrun. But not during full and new moons, when the stronger tides tear apart the boundary layer. Inertia also plays a role: The larger the bay or arm of the harbor, the longer it takes to respond to tidal changes by reversing flow.

Beyond the worldwide trend toward rising oceans, New York's sea level rises and falls with the seasons. Because of melting polar ice and the expansion of water volume as it warms, the average sea level in the harbor is about seven inches higher in August than in January. Tides in the harbor are moderate by international standards, with a typical range of five to six feet, and two high and two low tides per day. But the tidal range of the East River near the Battery is 4.4 feet; at the Long Island Sound end of the same strait it is 7.2 feet. Various arms of the harbor flush at unequal rates: the average time a parcel of water sloshes around before being carried out is thirty-five days in Jamaica Bay, fifteen days in the Hudson River during spring but more than forty-five in summer, and little more than twenty-four hours in the East River. Water may ride back and forth through the Arthur Kill for two weeks, the push and pull from its two ends so balanced that the direction of its net flow is still not definitively known. During typical spring high-flow conditions, fresh water reaches Manhattan and catfish can occur among anglers' catches; during droughts, saline waters intrude and marine fish may be caught at Peekskill some fifty-five miles up the Hudson.

Large artificial streams—sewer outfalls—join natural tributaries in jetting fresh water into the system at various points. The seagulls that routinely hover over a patch of roily water near Robbins Reef in the Upper New York Bay are searching for edible bits in a sewage-laden freshwater outfall routed all the way from the upper Passaic River in New Jersey. Indeed, the amount of fresh water entering the Arthur Kill from its two largest tributaries, the Rahway and Elizabeth Rivers, is dwarfed by the freshwater flow from sewage-treatment plants and industry. Even air pressure changes can alter the relationships among the different waterways that form the harbor, affecting flow and tidal swings.

Many have praised the moderate climate of the harbor. The Reverend Charles Wolley, writing of his stay from 1668 to 1670, described it as "of a sweet and wholesome breath, free from those annoyances which are commonly ascribed by Naturalists for the insalubriety of any Country, *viz.* South or South-east winds, many stagnant Waters, lowness of shoars, inconstancy of Weather, and the excessive heat of the Summer; the extremity of which is gently refresh'd, fann'd and allay'd by constant breezes from the Sea."

But ill winds may blow. A nor'easter, that big cyclone, drives water down Long Island Sound and the New York Bight, where it piles into the harbor and the Hudson River, often meeting a rush of rainwater draining from the Hudson Valley; the surge may rise several feet above normal, especially on a high tide. Dramatic flourishes are possible. Driving along the Brooklyn shore in a freakish October coastal storm that featured snow, sleet, and rain, I spotted a tall grayish column over the harbor—a waterspout, or waterborne tornado. And few are aware of the opposite situation to a flooding nor'easter. When a nor'wester howls down the Hudson River, particularly on a full- or new-moon low tide, water is driven out of the river—a "blowout tide"—revealing large portions of the bottom rarely seen and best avoided by harbor mariners.

Most worrisome are hurricanes. Although the Great Hurricane of 1938 that devastated eastern Long Island is the oft-cited local touchstone for potential consequences, Dr. Nicholas Coch of Queens College has revived interest in largely forgotten hurricanes that hit New York City in 1821 and 1893. In the 1893 storm the tide rose thirteen feet in one hour, and waters from the Hudson and East Rivers met across lower Manhattan. Waves reached at least twenty-five feet and eliminated Hog Island, a resort community between Rockaway and Long Beach. Coch predicts that a Category Three storm (two notches below a maximum-strength Category Five storm) tracking over northern New Jersey would raise sea level by twenty feet at the Statue of Liberty and thirty feet in Jamaica Bay. The loss of property and, perhaps, lives when this happens will be frightful.

But despite its sheltered nature, New York Harbor is not without its dangers even in calm weather, and not all the bodies that turn up in it drop in from land. In the summer of 1998 alone a graduate student working on a fish survey was lost from a capsized vessel near the George Washington Bridge and a father drowned when a sudden and vicious line storm (what the early Dutch settlers called *swadelen*, or "moving sweeps") flipped his sailboat in the Upper Bay. The Coast Guard station gets little rest from saving souls in this little inland sea. Alas, even they have their limits. When anglers found a seven-foot python floating down Lower New York Bay they called the Coast Guard. The terse reply: "We don't do snakes."

28

3

Ecologically, the harbor's regional geography lends it a diverse fauna and flora; there are more rare species and communities in the metropolitan area than anywhere else in the state. Northern and southern forms mingle because of the collision of climate zones, the pronounced seasonal changes, and the intermediate latitude (often crossed by migratory species moving north and south). The harbor also has many natural habitats created by the juncture of land and sea, adding variety to the mix. Surf meets sand at classic ocean beaches at Coney Island and Sandy Hook; freshwater wetlands drain to brackish marshes on Staten Island; bedrock slopes under the East River; sod banks and sandbars are washed by the tides in Jamaica Bay; mudflats line the Hackensack River; and desertlike high beach with prickly pear cactus lines part of the Gateway National Seashore in Brooklyn.

Over the course of the year seasonal changes turn the waters of New York Harbor into a climatic fulcrum. During winter the Hudson River, nestled in the continental land mass, ices as it becomes colder than the nearshore waters of the New York Bight, which is part of that vast heat reservoir, the Atlantic Ocean. The intervening harbor has intermediate temperatures, but during harsh winters large floes of ice from the Hudson drift into the Upper Bay. In often-colder colonial times ships from the Battery area were berthed during winter in Turtle Bay near Forty-seventh Street on the saltier East River to avoid the dangerous ice. In spring the river warms more quickly than the Atlantic and all three regions briefly equalize before the Hudson's temperature exceeds the ocean's, often reaching into the low eighties in August, some ten degrees higher than off Long Island. Temperatures balance again in autumn before settling back into the winter pattern.

These broad swings between warmth and chill have profound effects on the animals that live in the harbor and that pass through it in all directions. Diversity of life in the harbor peaks in early autumn and is lowest in winter. But even large mammals can be seen frolicking in the lower Hudson off Manhattan on January 1. The Coney Island Arctic Ice Bears, a group of masochistic swimmers, makes its annual New Year's Day swim in the Hudson River at Twenty-third Street in waters a few degrees above freezing.

2
VITA MARINAE

"If there is magic on this planet,
it is contained in water."

Loren Eisley
The Flow of the River (1957)

1

ON THE MAP NEWARK BAY is an armpit of New York Harbor, a geographical relationship fully consistent with its popular image. My own expectations of Newark Bay are in keeping with this view as we ready the trawl net at the stern of the *Gloria Michelle*, a research vessel operated by the U.S. National Marine Fisheries Service. The crew is documenting the fish composition of the bay, but I'm aboard to collect specimens for a survey of toxic contamination of New York Harbor's finfish and shellfish. A first take on Newark Bay does not bring its fishery resources to mind. The western shore is lined by deep shipping terminals—huge incisors that bite almost to the longitudinal navigation channel that sections the bay. Picketing the piers are lofty, birdlike cranes lifting containers from cargo ships. Trucks zoom everywhere on the surrounding roads. Oil tanks line much of the near shore, with the taller buildings of Newark and Manhattan filling in the sooty background. Newark Bay appears to be little more than an aesthetically forsaken floatage with a massive infrastructure designed to snatch society's necessities from seagoing vessels.

One of the scientists on board says, "We'll catch plenty of fish," adding that he also is surprised by the incongruity of habitat and habituate, but then how for cruise after cruise he has witnessed a remarkable assortment of sea life. As we idle northward the trawl is reeled to the channel bottom, and for five minutes its giant mouth gathers those creatures that fail to flare from its path. The net is landed and its cod-end opened. On this tow, and the next few, we catch a chair seat, a refrigerator packing box, a tree trunk, broken bottles, reams of decomposing paper, and an automobile tire that had been tagged previously by a crew member in an informal study of their numbers on the floor of Newark Bay.

Mixed with this refuse is a rich, flopping assemblage of marine animals. Snapper bluefish and porgies are included, October stragglers from their autumn migrations to the continental shelf. We catch striped bass, along with a newcomer to the Hudson, gizzard shad. Some remnants of the summer fauna are more reminiscent of the Chesapeake Bay: blue claw crabs and the young of four members of the drum family—weakfish, croakers, silver perch, and lafayettes. (Lafayettes are forever associated with the Marquis de Lafayette after one of the fish's cyclic population bursts coincided with the Frenchman's visit to New York City in 1824.) Cool-water species include tomcod, butterfish, hake, and sculpins. Menhaden, locally "mossbunker," enter the haul, together with sea robins, which

32

swim with winglike fins over the seafloor. Sharing the channel bottom with blue claw crabs are the primitive-looking relatives of spiders and trilobites—horseshoe crabs, avoided by virtually all of humankind except baymen, who know them to be the pièce de résistance as bait for their eel pots. Most intriguing are the mantis shrimp, stocky red crustaceans that live cryptically in burrows like underwater prairie dog colonies throughout Newark Bay and the rest of New York Harbor.

We trawl a series of stations northward to the mouth of the Hackensack River, where a condominium complex, a lonely and tenuous foothold of gentrification, provides a clear view of refinery tanks on the opposite bank and where the air smells like linseed oil. Next we survey the west shore of the Passaic River mouth, the former site of the Diamond Shamrock Company, whose chemical product, the defoliant Agent Orange, bequeathed the highest dioxin levels in the United States to the sediments near its underwater discharge pipes. This most toxic substance made by humans has not dissuaded blue claw crabs, for here we catch two bushels in one tow. Most are "jimmies," big, feisty males; the few female "sooks" stand out clearly because of their lustrous red-tipped claws. Agitated, they jab and snap indiscriminately, and when we lift one from the bucket a long daisy chain of prime, market-sized, but dioxin-ridden crabs follows.

The most hopeful beacon of the health of the present Newark Bay ecosystem is caught by accident at the confluence of the Passaic and Hackensack Rivers. Although not designed to harvest shellfish, the trawl net yields a single adult oyster, an environmentally sensitive and completely immobile creature that can close up for a time but can't escape from deleterious water quality; the oyster may be the best sentinel for the state of the harbor.

2

New York Harbor's vast network of moving or placid, fresh, brackish, and salt waters, marshes and mudflats, creeks and canals, and narrows and broad expanses is home to a native fauna second to no other temperate estuary. A Dutchman, Jasper Danckaerts, wrote in a still highly entertaining journal of his explorations around New York City during 1679 and 1680 that "it is not possible to describe how this bay swarms with fish, both large and small, whales, tunnies, and porpoises, whole schools of innumerable other fish, which the eagles and other birds of prey swiftly seize in their talons when the fish come to the surface." Tom Lake, a naturalist who lives for the river and who edits the annual *Hudson River Almanac*, has documented 206 fish species within its drainage north of the Battery. Of these, almost half occur in the harbor region, in addition to the many marine species that are seen periodically or as onetime strays south of the Battery.

Others count the fish, too. Cathy Drew is director of the River Project, a resilient cross between a marine biological field station and a Tribeca neighborhood clubhouse for the outdoor minded, based on Hudson River Pier 26. Once an avid diver, Drew suffered a near-fatal episode of nitrogen narcosis or the "bends," the aftereffects now keeping her above the waterline. But for more than a decade, with passion undiminished, Drew has advanced her dream of educating and involving the public in the environment of the harbor. The River Project has been underfunded and overly politicized in the heated battles over the future of Manhattan's waterfront; nonetheless Drew and her eclectic assortment of volunteers have managed to document the variety of local fish by maintaining a string of simple killifish traps in the pier's depths.

Although they rarely catch killifish, the River Project has registered some thirty-four other kinds of fish. Many of these are the mundane regulars such as cunner, tautog, and sea bass that one expects to lurk around the harbor. But sea horses are common at Pier 26, where they pick food off the pilings and mix with their close but more anguilliform relatives, pipefish. Drew also has caught young fish from southern climes—foureye and spotfin butterflyfish, more often seen on coral reefs. The butterflyfish are annual visitors, expatriates from the Gulf Stream that summer in the harbor and then, based on diver observations in clearer Barnegat Bay waters, perish in autumn as temperatures decline.

3

Although the rich and colorful fish life of a coral reef is often cited as an exemplar of biodiversity, the harbor's ichthyofauna represents a less obvious variety, but of a higher order. Dr. C. Lavett Smith, curator emeritus at the American Museum of Natural History, has stressed that although the total species count on a coral reef may be greater than in an estuary such as the Hudson, most coral reef fish belong to the same families and genera, principally the groupers, snappers, and butterflyfish, and many of these represent subtle variations on a shared body form. Conversely, although Drew has documented only thirty-five fish species under Pier 26, they belong to thirty genera and twenty-five families—a salting across a generous range of the evolution and blueprints of fishes.

The accumulation of organismic wealth in the harbor owes much to its function as a transition zone, an interchange among aquatic highways and cul-de-sacs of divergent ecologies and temperaments. Estuaries, in fact, support narrow residential faunas composed of species of admirable tolerances and high abundances;

the few animals that can cope with wide salinity and temperature swings prosper in the ambient organic richness. But it's the seasonal visitors that drive the diversity. Striped bass, American shad, and Atlantic sturgeon are the glamorous migrants that return from the ocean every spring, swimming under the Verrazano Narrows Bridge, past Ellis Island, and well up the Hudson River to procreate. If, during April, one could render the river transparent and peer to the bottom of the channel, the northward parade of anadromous fish would be staggering—one-hundred- to two-hundred-pound sturgeon would ride the bottom below pods of ten- to sixty-pound striped bass and great shoals of shad. Hundreds of thousands of miniature shad look-alikes, the river herring—alewives and bluebacks—also would enter the mix. Although most would leave the river soon after spawning, their progeny would flourish in the fertile soup of the central Hudson, the young shad and river herring exiting the system in autumn as an endless stream of minted silver forms.

During summer countless anchovies invade the estuary from the bight. The nearly transparent adults spawn almost daily, their proliferation drawing sharp-toothed bluefish and fluke to Manhattan waters and Spanish mackerel to the Lower Bay. Other primary fodder includes diminutive grass shrimp that kick through brackish waters, the slightly larger sand shrimp that prefer saltier tracts, and tiny curved crustaceans called amphipods that swarm on seaweed and detritus. Blue claw crab larvae drift from the bight to the estuary, and adult blue claws—the "beautiful swimmers" of Chesapeake fame—march throughout the harbor and northward as far as Albany.

Early in fall a small tuna, the false albacore, zooms just under the surface south of the Verrazano Narrows Bridge; later in the season sea herring, long the most valuable fish in the Atlantic Ocean, spread throughout the metropolitan waters. In winter the blue claw crabs bed down in the mud, but silver and red hake patrol the bottom, sometimes ambushed by anglerfish that lie in wait.

Oddballs and historical occurrences contribute to the lists. Strays that have only been seen once or twice include lumpfish, burrfish, ladyfish, cornetfish, bonefish, cobia, basking sharks, and flying gurnard. Then there are the difficult-to-explain dropouts— a few fish, such as red drum and a marine catfish, seen decades ago are almost never encountered today. Black drum, absent for a century, were the scourge of the Staten Island oyster planters and were commonly caught around Manhattan to weights of seventy pounds, the Harlem River and the Battery being prime locations. Sheepshead are no longer caught at Sheepshead Bay or anywhere else around New York City.

4

The oft-repeated notion that the Hudson once was a salmon river leads back to the river's namesake, Henry Hudson. As Hudson's ship, the *Halfmoon*, journeyed up the river in 1609, the master's mate, Robert Juet, wrote of the fish they observed. His notes included that they saw "many Salmons and Mullets and Rays very great" and "great store of salmons in the river." Some actual salmon were caught in the river from time to time, and this, together with the accounts from Hudson's voyage, led to the tempting thought that if the king of fish once ran in the Hudson River, they might again. Speculations on the cause of their decline ranged wildly, from too many steamboats to the polluting effects of sawdust in tributaries where they might have spawned.

Young Atlantic salmon were stocked in the Hudson River in

keeping with this dream and with the almost euphoric casting about of fish where they didn't belong in North America in the late 1800s that was an outgrowth of the great strides made in fish propagation at that time as well as the erection of the transcontinental rail system that allowed transport of "aquarium cars" from which live fish were stocked. Results were decidedly mixed. Atlantic lobsters and tautog did not take to the Pacific. Striped bass and American shad flourished there. Pacific chinook salmon were stocked in a Hudson tributary, Fishkill Creek near Poughkeepsie, in 1873 and 1876, and in the Raritan River in 1873, but to no avail.

Several million newly hatched Atlantic salmon young from eggs shipped from the Penobscot River in Maine were stocked in the Hudson during the 1880s. Enough returned from the sea to supplement commercial fishermen's catches—in one year more than three hundred adults, ten to thirty-eight pounds each, were taken in nets in the lower river (all contrary to law), and the first recorded catch by an angler occurred in 1888 at the foot of the dam at Troy. But the fishery never blossomed, salmon eggs became scarcer and more expensive, stocking declined and then ceased, and the Hudson's experimental flirtation with *Salmo salar* soon withered.

To bring back the lost salmon of the Hudson has remained a romantic fantasy that even fueled production of an off-Broadway play. But serious investigators have never found evidence for the existence of native salmon in the river. Even DeWitt Clinton researched the subject, concluding that the crew of the *Halfmoon* mistook striped bass for salmon. But it is more likely that they misidentified a different species. Dr. William Zeisel, an owlish historian and student of sportfishing who has studied the Hudson, noted that the actual Dutch words translated as "salmon"—*salm* and *salmpie*—were also used in common conversation for trout.

Perhaps the most similar fish (but not closely related) to trout in the Hudson estuary is the weakfish, which has a near relative with an almost identical profile that is not by chance called sea trout. And the timing of Henry Hudson's exploration of the river, early September, is often a period of great weakfish abundance. Records show that they fished on September 4, 1609, just inside Sandy Hook, a prime weakfishing location to this day.

5

What Henry Hudson and the colonists who followed did find were oysters in fantastic abundance. Long a mainstay of the Indians of the region, oyster beds stretched from Croton-on-Hudson to Raritan Bay—perhaps 350 square miles of shelled bottom. European settlers were soon eating oysters raw, broiled on coals, boiled in fat, and preserved in vinegar. One Dutch settler reported to the Hague, "Oysters we pick up before our fort . . .

Oystering at Prince's Bay, c. 1853. (Staten Island Historical Society)

Workers gathering oysters from a brackish creek at low tide in Keyport, New Jersey, c. 1910. Oysters were held in such creeks for about eighteen hours before being sold. (Keyport Historical Society)

some so large they must be cut up in two or three pieces." In 1753 the Swedish naturalist Peter Kalm observed that "there are poor people who live all year long upon nothing but oysters and a little bread." Regarded as an excellent winter food source, in 1715 oysters were prohibited from harvest in New York from May through August. Bedloe's Island, now called Liberty Island, was known as Oyster Island; two small reefs just south of it were called the Little Oyster Islands. In fact the Carwitham Map, depicting the harbor in 1730, shows the entire cove that forms the New Jersey shore of the Upper New York Bay as one gigantic oyster reef.

By 1800 there were oyster houses in lower Manhattan advertising "Jamaicas," "Rockaways," and "Amboys," named after the regional beds they were taken from. Street vendors sold them on

Manhattan oyster house. (Staten Island Historical Society)

the half shell. Saloons offered the "Canal Street Plan"—all the oysters you could eat for six cents—and they signaled fresh deliveries with big red muslin balloons. (If a customer became too greedy a bad oyster could be served to curb his appetite.) Oysters were made into soups, patties, and puddings, and eaten for breakfast, lunch, and dinner—in 1851 a traveler remarked, "Everyone here seems to eat oysters all day long." Two centers of oyster trade developed in lower Manhattan, one each on the Hudson and East Rivers. Both were made up of flat-bottomed scows docked side by side, known as "oyster rows." Oysters came in through the back doors and were sold through the front doors. Discarded shells abounded. Some were burned and turned into a form of lime used in building houses. Manhattan's Pearl Street was so named because it was originally "paved" with oyster shells. But the best use would have been to return them to the harbor bottom to maintain the continuity of the oyster reefs. The wisdom of this did not become apparent until about 1830, at City Island, near the East River's Long Island Sound terminus, where oystermen first began to replenish the shells on local beds.

Although a craze for the "luscious bivalves," as they were actually called, peaked in the United States in the mid- to late 1800s, oystering in New York Harbor declined because of overharvest, siltation stirred up by channel dredging, and increased pollution; however, in 1880 some 765 million oysters were still being harvested yearly from the waters around New York City, and 300 million as late as 1907, with annual per-capita consumption estimated at 660 oysters. But particular beds were gaining reputations for producing oysters that tasted like petroleum. Soon after, typhoid fever outbreaks from contaminated shellfish from Jamaica and Raritan Bays ended any lingering interest in consuming the remnants of the local oyster stocks.

If the oyster is the sentinel of the harbor, the striped bass is the harbor's symbol, a pin-striped tough guy that transcends its surroundings. Although some stripers wander the Northeast from the Bay of Fundy to the Chesapeake, many lead the life of wealthy Manhattanites, wintering on the Upper West Side and summering in the Hamptons. Ian Frazier described the bass as the perfect New York fish, with an urban glint to its eye; "if they could talk," he said, "they would talk fast." And like most New Yorkers, stripers stand their ground. Adam Brown, a commercial diver who has logged thousands of hours beneath the harbor's surface while performing inspections, often has to fight for space with bass. The problem is that bass gather behind structures in the same lee of the current that Brown needs to stay in so as not to be carried down the harbor. The fish were particularly difficult one day behind the Fifty-ninth Street Bridge abutments in the East River—a school of three-foot stripers jostled and banged Brown until he was reduced to hitting them back and cursing them through his mouthpiece.

Perhaps overly tolerant, striped bass are found everywhere within the harbor that oxygen levels allow. They thrive in sewage outfalls. Robert H. Boyle, in *The Hudson River: A Natural and Unnatural History*, discussed the sewer cognoscenti, anglers who specialize in fishing the dark discharges that spew from the many underground orifices that ring the city. On Martha's Vineyard fashionably outfitted fly-fishing sporties debate which combinations of exotic bird feathers should be bundled as flies to best "match the hatch" of that week's silvery baitfish; at the 125th Street sewer it's a question of whether to lob a juicy sandworm, a hunk of oily menhaden, or a bloody slice of beef liver.

Stripers become an obsession of anglers who are smitten by the challenge of catching a canny, discriminating warrior that can reach one hundred pounds and lives right in their neighborhoods, albeit a little below sea level. However, in a city not closely in tune with the recreational use of its waterfront, obtaining access to good striper-fishing locations is difficult. And first it may take overcoming prejudices and misconceptions.

Two of my high school friends, Steve Gabriel and Artie Smerz, grew up in Manhattan a few blocks from the East River in the east eighties, in the old German and Hungarian neighborhood of Yorkville. Smitten with stripers, they would lug their considerable gear to the northeast Bronx on treks that involved a subway ride, a bus ride, and a two-mile hike. For a long time they considered the

Angler landing striped bass near United Nations building. (Charles H. Traub)

East River suitable only for whisking away human wastes. One day they saw splashes on the river's surface and assumed that someone was throwing stones off the top of a building. When they realized the spreading rings were made by feeding stripers, they ran home for their rods and rarely visited the Bronx thereafter.

Some time later Smerz told me he had found a new spot in the East River he wanted to show me—one that necessitated a little physical and legal risk but that was worth it. He explained we needed to try the spot at night because once when he fished there during the day, someone assumed he must be attempting suicide and called 911. He soon found himself pinned between the flashing lights of a police car behind him and a police boat in front of him. On this night I followed him over a railing and onto FDR Drive, where we ran like guerrillas alongside the traffic to a concrete seawall. Sitting on the narrow barrier, Smerz and I dropped our lures between the pilings and instantly hooked into bass. But we couldn't control the frisky stripers we landed; some flopped onto the highway, where speeding cars weaved among fishermen and fish—an element of excitement that striper angling on Martha's Vineyard can't offer.

6

In the 1980s striped bass and other harbor dwellers were threatened by a suite of proposed waterfront development schemes driven by the Reagan economic boom and blessed by then-mayor Edward Koch. Because these projects required environmental impact reviews, government agencies were compelled to take greater notice of the harbor's collective heartbeats. In 1988 the U.S. Environmental Protection Agency, the New York State Department of Environmental Conservation, and the New Jersey

Department of Environmental Protection obtained a federal designation for the harbor complex as an Estuary of National Significance—a ranking that also delivered millions of federal dollars to be used for a management conference of these same agencies to restore and protect the metropolitan waters.

To qualify for this program a new, somewhat cumbersome geographical entity was conceived: the New York/New Jersey Harbor Estuary. The "harbor estuary" part was chosen to focus on the urban portion of the much larger Hudson River estuary, normally considered to encompass the harbor's waters, and the "New York/New Jersey" part to provide a politically correct twist and an even playing field for state-agency competition over what has always been known as New York Harbor.

In 1993 officials involved in the Harbor Estuary Program decided to acquire data on contamination levels of a lengthy list of the harbor's finfish and shellfish. I volunteered to lead an effort to acquire the samples as long as I could recruit some true harbor expertise—in particular my friend Captain Joe Shastay, a "harbor rat" in the most exalted sense of the term. Captain Joe is owner of a unique niche in the angling world—he is the only professional angling guide dedicated to gamefishing in New York Harbor. I first met Shastay after he telephoned me, looking for a study of striped bass he could perform as a senior thesis in college. A true straight arrow—husband, hunter, angler, and general outdoorsman—at that time Shastay was contemplating one of life's inexplicable sets of choices: whether to become a fishing guide or a chiropractor.

Shastay chose the angling life. He runs one or two charters per day, crossing the mouth of the Hudson in his outboard boat from a Jersey City marina to pick up bankers and brokers at various

Landing a large bluefish in the East River. Captain Joseph Shastay is holding the fish. (John Waldman)

landings around Manhattan. His knowledge of the harbor bottom is unsurpassed: He knows which tidal stage will produce striped bass, bluefish, or weakfish at any location, and what lure or bait will seduce them. Although Shastay fishes the commonly known spots as well or better than anyone else, it is his ability to cull fish from secret places that causes other boaters to stalk him. When the fishing is slow Shastay might confidently instruct his charges to plunk a lure into a three-foot gap between two moored barges or to cast behind the fourth piling in a series and count to twelve before retrieving, thereby manufacturing at least a modest catch from scattered schools.

Before he began taking clients, Shastay spent several years learning the city's waters on his own time while patching together a living on land. One November day during this period he and I joined a small fleet drifting the channel near Ellis and Liberty Islands. The bite started slowly, but as the tide began to ebb great schools of stripers stacked up in the wash of the Hudson River, feeding on its out-migrating wealth of fish. Every descent of our lures resulted in a strike from hellbent-on-eating striped bass. We fought long battles with the scrappy stripers, and many among the Upper Bay's never-ending traffic of pleasure craft, police vessels, tour boats, and tugs took notice and waved. Our most appreciative audience, though, lined the rails of the passing Staten Island Ferry. As we landed another pair of bass the entire port-side crowd broke into cheers and applause, upon which we bowed deeply, releasing the fish as our encore. At dusk the buildings of lower Manhattan lit up, dazzling us with a vertical cascade of lights. Such is the unique charm of Manhattan striped bass fishing.

Our goal in the agencies' contamination study was to collect more than seven hundred specimens of twenty-two species, some in several size classes, from a harbor arbitrarily divided into five regions. We fished mainly with hook and line, rotating through these areas to intercept the seasonal changes in the fauna. Shastay and I fished alone or together, all over the harbor. Some categories on the docket came easily, such as Captain Joe's specialty, striped bass and bluefish. One drizzly October day we had guests, quality-control inspectors from two of the agencies involved in the study. We took them up the East River to a reef just off U Thant Island, the little man-made knob south of Roosevelt Island and not far from the southernmost natural rock outcrop of the entire New England coast, near the Fifty-ninth Street Bridge. As we anchored we heard the watery chop of bluefish jaws savaging baitfish. Each of us fed lures into the flow, and all were pounced upon by hefty bluefish and stripers that ran deep and fought hard in the swift current. The inspectors, both angling novices, were awed by the quarry and their location, the sheer escarpment of the United Nations building and the roily waters providing the feeling of being in an urban Grand Canyon. And we passed our inspection.

Shastay and I hadn't expected to find oysters throughout the harbor, but my accidental catch in Newark Bay inspired us to look harder for them. I searched for oysters in all four corners of Jamaica Bay, a spot that was brimming with other kinds of life. A few stabs of a shovel in the low-tide sands near the Cross Bay Boulevard Bridge produced dozens of cherrystones—amazingly abundant because the contaminated clams were off limits to harvest. The channel bottoms were dotted with fluke, above which swam squadrons of hungry sea robins and swarms of porgies. A tropical banded rudderfish played hide-and-seek under my boat. And I found that oysters had lived in Jamaica Bay. One day in Mill Basin, a tidal creek leading to the bay, I let my skiff drift with the wind on an especially low tide. Peering over the side, I saw that the bottom had once been home to great numbers of magnificent oysters—eight- to ten-inch-long shells were everywhere, but not a live oyster could be seen anywhere. How long ago they lived there, no one could tell me.

But oysters do inhabit crevices among the rocks of the seawall at the Battery. Oysters can be found on the bottom of the Arthur Kill. Oysters live in the East River. On an afternoon low tide I went to College Point on the north shore of Queens County and visited MacNeill Park, one of New York City's unsung green places. Expecting to gather the commonplace mussels and soft-shell clams, as I nosed around I noticed cryptic brown forms clinging to the boulders—oysters camouflaged with silt. Not stacked on top of each other fighting for space as they do in oyster havens like

A shark attack just above the narrows in July 1880, inspired this illustration. (*Seaport* magazine)

the Carolinas, but distributed here and there among the rocks, at a density somewhere between that of early pioneers and established homesteaders.

The impetus for the toxics survey was concern about consumption of fish caught in the growing recreational fisheries of the harbor. To many, sportfishing in New York Harbor waters is an oxymoronic phrase associated with reeling in used condoms, aka Coney Island whitefish. The comedian Robert Klein defines optimism as fishing in the Hudson River. But there is a surprisingly rich tradition of angling in the city's waters, chronicled best by William Zeisel. Among his findings was the regular presence until the middle of the nineteenth century of sharks along Manhattan's commercial waterfront, particularly the East River. Not little sharks, but eight- and twelve-footers, drawn to the shallows by the raw refuse of the markets and common enough that one market worker, well known for overpowering sharks with the customary tug-of-war gear of handheld rope tied to chain, landed seven in one day. A woodcutting exists of a scene from the foot of Vesey Street in August 1881 in which a ten-foot shark is being hauled over the side of a dock as bystanders scatter in fear and one man points a pistol toward the shark's head. Only a year earlier a school of sharks had attacked a sailboat in the Verrazano Narrows; the captain fought them off with a wooden seat ripped from the vessel. Zeisel speculates that the near absence of sharks in the harbor since the turn of the century was due to increasing industrial contamination of the waters overwhelming their sensitive sense of smell—their main means of finding food.

Zeisel considers New York City to have become the capital of American angling by 1850. Skiffs were available for rent at locations such as a barge at Whitehall Street at a charge of $0.25 an hour or $1.50 a day, and during summer hundreds of boats fished all over the harbor. Good striped bass fishing was available in Newtown Creek and the Harlem River (the latter was temporarily blockaded by a series of milldams), but Hell Gate in the East River was widely regarded as the finest spot. Anglers rented rowboats at creeks that ran west to Lexington Avenue and then braved currents that were the bane of larger commercial vessels. It was with ample justification that the name Hell Gate was awarded. During the mid-1800s approximately one thousand ships ran aground annually on Hell Gate's notorious reefs—about one of every fifty that attempted passage, most notably the British frigate *Hussar,* which took several million dollars' worth of gold down with her to the bottom of the East River. A map of Hell Gate from 1777 shows a narrow and shallow channel studded with bedrock fingers and ledges that became famous for the damage they inflicted.

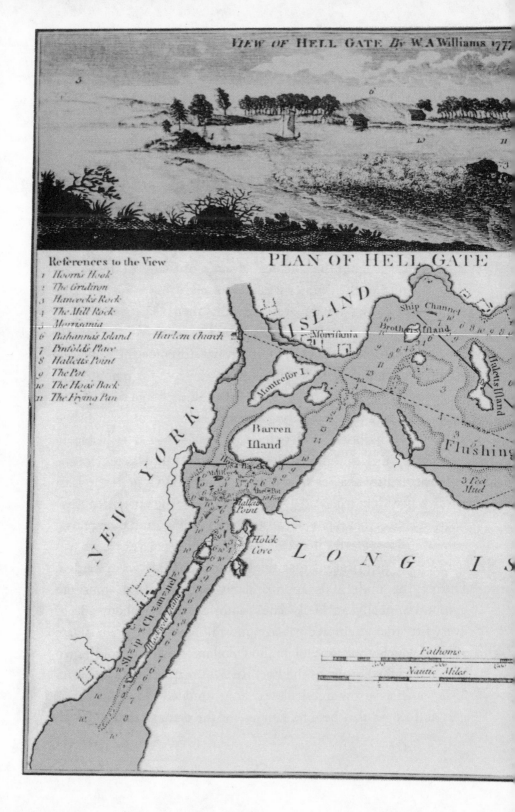

VIEW OF HELL GATE *By W.A.Williams* 1777

PLAN OF HELL GATE

References to the View

1 Hoorn's Hook
2 The Gridiron
3 Hancock's Rock
4 The Mill Rock
5 Morisania
6 Buhannas Island
7 Pinfold's Place
8 Hallett's Point
9 The Pot
10 The Hog's Back
11 The Frying Pan

ISLAND

Harlem Church

Morisania

Ship Channel

Brothers Island

Hallets Island

NEW YORK

Montresor I.

Barren Island

Flushing

Hog's Back

Mill

the Pot

3 Feet Mud

Hallet Point

Holck Cove

LONG IS

Sharp Channel

Hudsons Rising

Fathoms

Nautic Miles

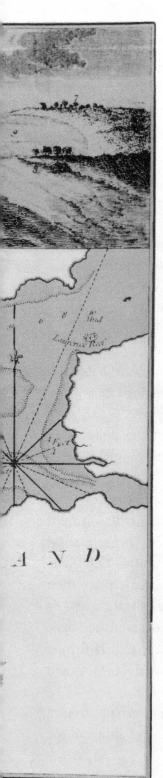

Map of Hell Gate showing major reefs, 1777.

The gauntlet included Heel Tap, Bread and Cheese, Hen and Chicken, Hogs Back, Negro Head, Frying Pan, and the Pot, among others. A whirlpool there made such a roar that sailors could hear it at a quarter of an hour's distance.

The 1777 Plan of Hell Gate offered instructions to mariners reminiscent of a whitewater rafting guidebook:

> *Hell Gate* and the Narrow pafs leading into Long Island Sound, at the time of Slack Water and with a leading Wind, may safely be attempted by Frigates. Small Ships and Vefsels with a commanding Breeze pafs at all times, with the Tide. On the Flood, bound into the *Sound* you pafs to the Southward of *Flood Rock*, which is the southernmost of the Three Remarkable Rocks in the pafsage. On the Ebb you go to the Northward of the *Mill Rock*, the Stream of the Tide setting that way, and forming Eddies in the *Flood Pafsage*, which is at that time very unsafe. *The Pot* on which there is 10 Feet at Low water shows itself distinctly by the Whirlpools, as also the *Paw* which is a part of the *Hogs Back*.

One need only view kayakers practicing today on the since-tamed remaining rapids at Hell Gate to appreciate how perilous it must have been. Dreamland, the turn-of-the-century theme park at Coney Island, had a turbulent water ride named after Hell Gate. Striped bass favor tide rips, because strong currents place their much smaller prey at a disadvantage. Hell Gate's shoals, swept by tides as fast as ten knots, drew striped bass in grand numbers. Guides manned the oars as their patrons trolled; anglers fishing alone held their lines in their mouths as they rowed. To withstand strikes, solo anglers had to have their original teeth.

Blasting of its reefs has slowed Hell Gate's currents from a scary ten knots to a still-respectable five knots. And although the

Striped bass fishing in Hell Gate, c. 1869.

boat liveries are long gone, Hell Gate remains a superior place to
catch striped bass. In fact the unofficial New York City–record
striper of sixty-four pounds was pulled from its depths by *New
York Times* photographer Keith Myers.

The Shermans, a Brooklyn-based family, are among the most
ardent of New York Harbor anglers. Ben, a doctor, and his four sons,
also doctors, have for decades relaxed by chasing stripers throughout
New York City waters, sometimes catching hundreds in a day.
Although they sometimes fish Hell Gate, one of their favored locations is farther up the East River, alongside the pier that extends into
Flushing Bay from La Guardia Airport. Not only is the fishing great
there, but they can also experience the roar, turbulence, and heat of
727s and other jets taking off not far above their heads.

But despite the ample supply of fish, government agencies have
shown a pronounced ambivalence concerning angling in metropolitan waters. Managers have debated whether to advance the

cause of fishing by increasing waterfront access—this would promote consumption of contaminated fish but at the same time concentrate fishermen and, via signs, educate them as to the risks involved—or whether to do nothing, in effect discouraging fishing. The former attitude seems to prevail, and limited access for anglers has been provided at sites around the harbor. However, much of the fishing that occurs at public access locations and the many ill-defined interstitial spaces along the waterfront is of a subsistence nature, most often by people who don't always pay attention to harvest regulations. But enforcement of these regulations is also lax, partly because it is difficult to be unsympathetic to such a direct grasp at protein.

Then there are those who poach for profit from the city's waters. One damp October day Shastay and I spotted a boat due south of the Battery with four anglers, who appeared to be landing at least one fish at any moment. We anchored downcurrent of them and enjoyed superb angling; every drop of our lines resulted in magnificent ten- to twenty-pound striped bass and bluefish. But we noticed that the vessel's crew was not releasing any stripers, an obvious violation of the law given the one-fish-per-angler limit. The fish were being kept in a weighted mesh bag alongside the boat, ready to be cut away if anyone suspicious approached. They were pinhookers—fishermen who angle for profit, in this case illegally.

The economic incentives to poach are strong. In the early 1980s New York State raised the minimum length of harvestable striped bass from sixteen to twenty-four inches at a time when fishermen were permitted to keep unlimited numbers of them. An article in the *New York Times* stated that just before the law went into effect, one fisherman who made a very good living pinhooking had caught 150 stripers in one day near the Statue of Liberty, most measuring eighteen to twenty-two inches. He sold that catch for fourteen hundred dollars. When he went out again under the new regulations he caught 111 stripers, of which 108 had to be released. He said, "It felt like throwing $10 bills into the air."

The temptation to catch and pass off, illegally, very abundant fish and shellfish from contaminated waters to unsuspecting buyers is one that some find irresistible. The New York State Department of Environmental Conservation maintains a small but well-trained Marine Enforcement Unit that patrols the waters and checks the fish markets. Sometimes their results are spectacular. One December night in 1997 conservation officers spied a boat with two men clamming in Mott Basin, a polluted backwater of Jamaica Bay, near Kennedy Airport. The patrolmen watched for an hour and saw that the clams were so plentiful, it took the efforts of both men to lift the loaded clam rake back into the boat. When the officers moved in, the poachers dumped the clams overboard and jetted toward Rockaway Inlet and the ocean. Reaching a speed of forty-five miles per hour, the poachers led a parade of police, Coast Guard, and other agency vessels, emergency vehicles on shore, and finally two helicopters on a thirty-one-mile chase up the East River and through Hell Gate before they began to run out of gas, fittingly, near Rikers Island. As a final act they tried to ram their boat into a Department of Corrections chase vessel. Had they not been found, they might have taken and sold ten to twenty bushels at one hundred to two hundred dollars apiece for a night's work, eventually making some lovers of raw clams extremely ill. Instead the two—dedicated clam poachers for twenty years and believed to be part of an interstate ring of illegal clammers—were charged with resisting arrest, reckless endangerment, possession of a stolen engine, and poaching.

Conservation officers also nailed a striped bass poaching ring in Jamaica Bay with a sting operation. Posing as a fish buyer who had "restaurant contacts," an undercover officer bought, over several weeks and for two thousand dollars, 686 pounds of mostly undersized striped bass taken from waters where commercial harvest is banned because of contamination. The poachers faced penalties of $270,000 and four years in jail. But sometimes poaching busts are comically accidental. Driving by coincidence behind a white box truck on the Brooklyn-Queens Expressway, two officers wondered why their windshield was being pelted with slime oozing from the vehicle ahead. They pulled the truck over and discovered wet tubs full of fish, including thirty-two undersized tautog.

Traditional commercial fishing has been pushed to the very limits of the harbor. The March 1947 *National Geographic* featured an article on the shad fishermen across the river from Manhattan who "fished in the shadow of skyscrapers." Professionals, often Scandinavian and Portuguese itinerants who worked their way from fishery to fishery along the coast and the Great Lakes, would show up at Fort Lee during April to join crews that lived on barges and fished assigned "rows" along the Jersey side. They were so good at fishing that one shad camp operator said, "They know how to do almost any commercial fishing—and if they don't they can pick it up between breakfast and lunch and do it better by supper than the ones who taught them." During those bounteous times fifty-five rows were fished at fifteen-hundred-foot intervals between Sixtieth Street, Manhattan, and the border between New Jersey and New York. In the 1800s a Brooklyn family operated a large shad-fishing operation in the Verrazano Narrows. To the north at Robbins Reef, near the mouth of the Kill Van Kull, were the "hedges"—rows of brush stuck in the shallows to steer shad toward nets. Today only Ron Ingold, present patriarch of an old shad-fishing family, fishes opposite Manhattan; the nearest shad-fishing operation northward is not found until the Tappan Zee Bridge, fourteen miles upriver.

7

If you cross the George Washington Bridge from Manhattan, travel a short distance south along the Hudson where the Palisades trail off and far too many apartment buildings and houses are jammed onto the cliffs, and then make a left turn down a short dirt road, you enter another place and time, the fishing camp of Ron Ingold. On his little peninsula stacks of fish traps are surrounded by nets, buoys, lumber, barrels, milk crates, anchors, engines, docks, and small shacks, much of the wooden infrastructure salvaged from what drifts by on the river. At its center is Ron's shanty, a two-room

Shad-fishing camp, Fort Lee, New Jersey. (John Waldman)

structure that has very few amenities but includes two husky guard dogs that interpret their mission broadly—one of them once urinated on the leg of a cable television salesman who quoted Ron too high a price for service. In front of the main shack are numerous floating piers, linked toward the river in an attempt to reach enough water to float his two old skiffs at low tide. Aquatic Appalachia comes to mind. But sit on a recliner on the deck in the summer sun and look downriver over the ship traffic and above the Hudson's rippling surface at Manhattan's skyline and you begin to feel the attraction of the place, the pull that keeps Ingold men maintaining this atavistic existence in a world ever less receptive to it.

The shad run was long since past and the mood relaxed when I visited the Ingold encampment. Shad season imparts a sense of urgency to early spring as the eager-to-spawn shad enter the river from the ocean and its few remaining fishermen hustle to suspend their nets at time-proven locations to intercept them. Sometime in March the Ingold crew pulls sixty-foot-long shagbark hickory stakes from the mud bottom of their cove in the river and drives them about half their length into the sediments under the New Jersey side of the George Washington Bridge. Shagbark hickory is preferred because of its density; at fifty-two pounds per cubic foot, it barely floats. Gill nets are stretched across the stakes and then tended every six hours during the short slack periods between the flood and ebb tides. The beginning of the run varies with springtime's pacing; it's said that when the buds on trees are as big as a mouse ear, the shad are in the river. The blooming of forsythia or "shadbush" also is a good indicator. The shad—big, silvery, commercially valuable herring that can reach about twelve pounds—are picked out of the nets, but in ever-dwindling numbers compared to the striped bass; the latter are presently unmarketable because of contamination with polychlorinated biphenyls (PCBs), and their abundance only seems to rise these days. Still, shad catches were sometimes great in the old days; one of Ingold's lifts totaled ten thousand pounds and left only three inches of free-board on the skiff.

The Ingolds' operation is also a relict in space; Ron's father once owned four fishing camps on the river, employing twenty-seven fishermen and three cooks. But Ron's and his son Scott's enthusiasm for the life and the locale still comes through. Despite health problems, fewer and fewer fish, and more and more restrictions, the sweet-natured Ron and more aloof Scott love to share their knowledge and theories of how the river works. And stories of what they've seen and know: how a stuck climber was airlifted off a nearby Palisades cliff, which shoreline house Geraldo Rivera's son lives in, and that ill-fated workers were once buried alive in the New Jersey–side stanchion of the George Washington Bridge.

They complain about the ever-present but legally unmarketable striped bass. Stripers are the shad fisherman's bane; not only do they mock their efforts in their plentitude and high commercial value, but they have sharp fin and gill spines that get stuck in the mesh and take much time to free up and release, cutting hands in the process. But when the crews return to shore with whatever shad are available, there are always ready buyers, pleased to partake in the ritual of dining on Hudson shad and, in particular, skeins of its precious roe.

Obtaining the roe is the easy part of the process: just slit the abdominal cavity. But boning a shad in order to prepare its meat is an abstruse art practiced today by a select few "boners." Much like another almost lost talent—the building of mortarless stone walls—it looks simple, but just try it. The experience of eating shad, a downright tasty fish (its Latin name, *Alosa sapidissima*, means "most delicious of herrings"; it perhaps is best enjoyed at a traditional shad bake, at which fish are split and nailed with bacon strips to an oaken plank facing an open fire), can be ruined if the fish isn't boned right. A human skeleton has 206 bones; a shad contains at least 500 more, not counting the intermuscular bones, and many are as fine as hairs.

Crab season follows shad season and extends until autumn. Unlike the Hudson's shad, which have shown a progressive decline since the nineteenth century (tied in some degree to spawning success within the river), the abundance of blue claw crabs fluctuates from year to year, dependent on the breeding fortunes of the great mid-Atlantic coastal crab population, the young crabs invading bays and rivers, with the Hudson forming the northernmost concentration of any consequence. When I arrived at Ingold's camp, Ron was about to deliver bushels of live crabs to New York and New Jersey fish markets and restaurants, the eventual consumers of which might automatically associate their dinners with the Chesapeake, not with the far less evocative if not downright off-putting Hudson River. The crabs are caught in traditional crab traps baited with seasoned menhaden (corrupted from the Indian word for fertilizer, *munnawhatteaug*). The mossbunker is an extremely oily herring that is salted and packed in drums, from which emerge months later potent-smelling slabs of fish flesh with the bronze glow of the "bog people," those unfortunate souls occasionally found buried in peat for centuries.

I went to Ingold's camp mainly to see the fieldwork on a study of the American eel, certainly one of the most unique species of fish in a taxonomic regime rife with peculiarities. Similarly to blue claw crabs, eels invade Atlantic coast rivers as young from the sea, but only after hatching near the center of the Atlantic Ocean, somewhere in the fathomless depths of the Sargasso Sea, an enormous and largely becalmed region of floating sargassum weed jungles and ultraclear water. Carried along North America by the Gulf Stream for a year or so, young transparent eels, called elvers, restock inshore waters annually, where they transform to their dark, juvenile phase. Males tend to remain in saline and brackish habitats, but females wriggle inland toward fresh water, passing through cracks in dams and even coursing over damp grass to reach lakes and ponds. Both sexes then pause a decade or more before descending to the ocean, migrating back to spawn and finally die in the Sargasso Sea—a life history that is a reverse image of the Pacific salmon's, albeit one that is more cryptic.

Dr. David Secor, a fish ecologist with the Chesapeake Biological Laboratory, had shaken his midwestern roots and become inspired to work on the diadromous fishes—those complicated species (including eels, salmon, shad, and striped bass) that journey between fresh and salt waters. To capture eels en masse, an arcane endeavor, Secor had hired the Ingolds for assistance and more than a little instruction. Scott Ingold headed us north in a thoroughly used skiff to lines of eel pots that had been baited and set on the bottom near the west side of the George Washington Bridge. We enjoyed a terrific view across the river and below the bridge of the hidden but far-from-forgotten Jefferies Hook Lighthouse, more commonly known as the Little Red Lighthouse, after Swift's and Ward's time-honored *The Little Red Lighthouse and the Great Gray Bridge*. Not far to the north, on the Bronx side of the Spuyten Duyvil, stands a statue of Henry Hudson—sadly disregarded since it was enveloped by condominiums—as the quadricentennial anniversary of his visit in 1609 approaches.

The pots were retrieved one by one and most had several eels in them, distinctly nervous individuals seduced by the siren-stench of the pickled bunker that followed the V-shaped mouths to enter the traps, then couldn't solve the funnel exits from their spouts back on out. Secor dosed the eels with a light narcotic to be able to handle them efficiently, a squirming, slime-covered eel being nearly impossible to hold. Even the age-old "eel grip"—middle finger wrapped tightly around one side of the fish's body, surrounding fingers braced on its other side—buys only a few seconds before the eel slips out.

Eels are designed for exploring the limits of the waters they inhabit and have the curiosity of cats, entering any opening, natural or man-made. Perhaps the quintessentially urban form of eel fishing was observed in the 1960s by Cyrus Adler, leader of the Shorewalkers, a New York City group. Late one night Adler noticed a man smoking a pipe and sitting next to an open manhole cover in Manhattan, two blocks inland from the East River. The man hauled a rope out of the sewer, at the end of which was an umbrella. He let the water drain from the umbrella, turned it over and poured a mess of eels into a crate, and then lowered the umbrella to "fish" again.

One of the purposes of the study was to estimate to what extent eels move once they are in the Hudson, that is, their local "home range." To accomplish this Secor had been marking them with freeze brands made icy with liquid nitrogen, etching a single block capital letter on their flanks to signify capture at a particular location over a particular period. I was surprised to see that about half of the eels we caught already bore letters on their sides, suggesting a high degree of residency for these fish. But I was struck by the eventual ramifications as individual eels acquired multiple marks, the possibility being that some eels might begin to spell words such as CAT, or maybe even GOD, perhaps causing some unsuspecting fisherman to claim that a divine miracle had occurred in the Hudson's waters.

8

What is clear from spending time on New York Harbor is that commercially valuable fish and shellfish are there—it's just that harvest is hostage to their contamination. And the fish were always there. Danckaerts wrote, "It is not necessary for those who live in the city [of New York] to go to the sea to fish, but they can fish in the river and waters inside; or even to the Great Bay [Upper New York Bay] and they can by means of *fuycks* [a stationary net] or seines not only obtain enough fish for their daily consumption, but also to salt, dry, and smoke, for commerce, and to export by the shiploads if they wish, all kinds of them, as the people of Boston do; but the people here have better land than they have there, where they have therefore resort more for a living to the water."

Because of contamination, most legal commercial fishing in the harbor is done at its edges, where polluted waters are diluted by the ocean or other, cleaner water bodies. To the south of Manhattan lobstering still occurs in the Upper Bay near the Verrazano Narrows Bridge, and crabbing at the mouth of the Kill Van Kull. Jamaica Bay once supported more than forty full-time dragger vessels that fished offshore and thousands of men who worked the bay; now there are two draggers and but a half-dozen baymen. Remuneration for the baymen comes from eels sold for food and bait, and from menhaden, killifish, and worms peddled to bait shops. One of the baymen, Karl Kirchner, still traps muskrats for their fur and their musk sacs, used to make perfume. Muskrat

HEARTBEATS IN THE MUCK

numbers have declined, but fewer than twenty years ago his operation bagged as many as eight hundred in a season.

Present large-scale commercial operations are restricted to the southern lip of the harbor in Belford, an insular and clannish port nestled in the marshy rim of Raritan Bay. The Belford fishermen are ghostly reminders of a time when Raritan Bay was a major seafood source, providing as much as one-fifth of the fifty to sixty million pounds of fish sold annually at the Fulton Fish Market. An exhaustive list of fish and shellfish was caught in the bay, with virtually every kind of gear used in coastal waters—including haul seines, pound nets, fyke nets, purse seines, otter trawls, pots, handlines, and even rakes and spears—used to pull eels out of the winter mud. Raritan Bay is also unique along the Atlantic coast in its supporting commercial fisheries for both blue claw crabs and lobsters. (In 1748 Peter Kalm was told by several individuals that European colonists had never seen or caught lobsters in the New York area and ate lobster only when they were shipped in wellboats from New England, until one of the well-boats broke in pieces near Hell Gate, stocking the region with breeding lobsters.) Fishermen of Raritan Bay enjoyed an unusual windfall during World War II. The U.S. government installed a metal net between Staten Island and Long Island to protect New York City from German submarines. The submarine net steered migrating shad toward the Staten Island shore, where pound nets temporarily made large catches.

Not noted for their obsequiousness to legalities, and emboldened by the scarcity of harvestable fish in the New York Bight, a portion of the "Belford pirates" fleet was nabbed several summers ago in a multiagency enforcement operation as they trawled illegally for fluke at night, in the Lower New York Bay. But even some conservation officers expressed understanding of the fishermen's plight. The boats that violate the law are typically small wooden vessels in disrepair that would be in danger in rough seas. Trawling in the safety of the bay but in violation of the law can generate perhaps five hundred to fifteen hundred dollars' worth of fish per night. Captain Ed Markowski of the enforcement division of the New Jersey Department of Environmental Protection said, "I can understand their dilemma. They are breaking the law. But they have to feed their family. I'm not sympathetic to what they're doing. But I am sympathetic to their overall plight."

The Fulton Fish Market in lower Manhattan, for more than 160 years the largest wholesale market for fish in the world, still received local catches by ship until the late 1970s. Today all of the seafood sold there arrives by truck, much of its former dockage occupied by the South Street Seaport and Pier 17—essentially shopping malls on stilts despite their nautical trimmings. A recent notion—a New York City–based port for fishing vessels to unload their holds efficiently to the New York markets—was an utter failure. Although Fishport, built by the Port Authority in the mid-1980s in Brooklyn's Erie Basin, was a state-of-the-art processing and distribution facility, few boats visited it; there just weren't enough fish to catch anymore in the once-rich waters of the nearby New York Bight. Ironically, in the reviving harbor there probably was no shortage of fish swimming beneath Fishport's berths.

9

Among the most glorious renaissances performed by the creatures of New York Harbor has been that of its wading birds. Sometimes referred to snidely as part of the "charismatic megafauna" by biologists who can't get the same attention for some less revered animals they study, the primary wading birds of the harbor include green herons; yellow-crowned and black-crowned night-herons; great, snowy, and cattle egrets; and glossy ibis. They nest in large numbers around its shores, but only in certain locations—within an archipelago of largely forgotten islands in the Arthur Kill and East River—that have fallen into disuse. Free of humans, raccoons, and other predators, these islands support now thriving colonies of wading bird species that in some instances have rebounded from near extinction and in others were never known to nest anywhere near New York City.

Nationally, millions of wading birds were slaughtered in the late 1800s for their feathers, which were used to adorn women's hats. The long plumes of great egrets were most prized. New York Harbor was not spared this madness. As recently as 1960 no egrets or ibis nested in the harbor. Peter Mott, president of the New York City Audubon Society, was quoted as saying that the mere sighting of an ibis in 1950 "was so unusual that I played hooky just to see one." In the late 1960s the kills were found to be devoid of aquatic organisms because of anoxic conditions. But with improvements in water quality and the consequent increase in forage fish populations, harbor heron numbers exploded, rising by one hundred pairs per year between the mid-1970s and mid-1980s. Today about 250 pairs of ibis nest on the harbor islands, and about the same number of each of the three egrets. The two kinds of night-herons total about two thousand breeding pairs. These not-long-ago nonexistent populations now represent about one-quarter of all the nesting wading birds between Cape May, New Jersey, and Rhode Island.

I have come to Elizabeth, a backwater town on the New Jersey side of the Arthur Kill, with Dr. Paul Kerlinger to see where the

Oystercatchers flying over a Jamaica Bay marsh. (Don Riepe, National Park Service)

harbor herons nest and to survey neotropical migratory songbirds. "Neotropical" because these slight animals, about an ounce in weight, travel seasonally between temperate North America and tropical Central America and South America. Kerlinger attempts to survey four or five successional stages of vegetation from grassland to adult forest; a consultant, he manages the harbor-related bird surveys for the New York City Audubon Society, including the Harbor Herons Program. (*Harbor herons* is a catchall phrase for the various wading birds.) On this flawless early-autumn morning we cross the Arthur Kill in a motorboat near where it meets Newark Bay and the Kill Van Kull and receive a grand view of a waterway that has suffered a thousand industrial slashes. But as we tuck the boat among the decaying timbers of a sunken barge and step onto Shooters Island (Schutters Island to the Dutch who hunted there), we are instantly in another world. Here and there sit the steel and wood remains of the isle's previous existence, including the drydocks, piers, and abandoned hulls of its once "monstrous shipyards," which endured from colonial times until they were deserted about seventy-five years ago. But Shooters Island's latest reincarnation is really a return to its earliest one—as a wild place. Inconveniently located near the main shipping channel, all fifty-one acres of Shooters Island were destined to be blasted away after maritime interests petitioned the Army Corps of Engineers to remove it. But recolonization by wading birds saved Shooters Island. How could New York Harbor afford to lose such an important heron rookery?

I sink the boat's anchor into the island's beach, which from a distance looked like some exotic reddish sand but which turns out

Staten Island beach with oyster shells and glass. (Ben Longstreth, Baykeeper)

to be almost all finely ground coal clinkers. We hike on faint trails through dense brush, passing a long-forgotten truck buried in a thicket like a battleground relict. Kerlinger pauses and makes sounds with his mouth to call birds—odd sucking, smacking, and screeching noises that would be socially unacceptable in any other setting. The response is underwhelming, but only because we are near the end of the migration season for neotropical songbirds. Although the birding is slow, most of our five-minute stops at each station in various habitat types reveal one or two "neotrops" and other less migratory aviators, including the American redstart warbler, ruby-crowned kinglet, catbird, and house wren.

Sometimes weather and migrational urges conspire to create sensational birding along New York Harbor's shores. May 19, 1996, was the best day in recorded history for spotting neotropical birds at the Jamaica Bay Wildlife Refuge. A coastal storm had stalled to the south of New York City and blocked the flyway for several days. The skies then cleared and released swarms of neotrops that had backed up on the southern edge of the disturbance. On this Sunday the foliage of the refuge was filled with all kinds of warblers back on the move: black-and-white, Canada, yellow, redstart, prairie, bay-breasted, blackpoll, and Blackburnian, among others. Early birders made excited phone calls that this was a day not to be missed, initiating a second migration, this time by car, and by afternoon the paths among the bushes were filled with enraptured bird-watchers.

Birders can get carried away when an unusual bird visits the harbor. Notice went out on the New York City Rare Bird Alert in late August 1998 that a single broad-billed sandpiper from the other side of the Atlantic was in town. Hundreds of telescope carriers, some from as far as California, descended on the Jamaica Bay

71

Wildlife Refuge hoping to glimpse the drab, seven-inch-long visitor and add an alien to their life lists. Perhaps one must be an ornithologist or serious birder to understand the fuss over this little accident of nature. As Dave Avrin, the refuge manager, said, "It could leave at any time. That's what makes this so exciting."

Although the harbor herons have been well studied, they can still perplex. The first nesting egrets were spotted on Shooters Island in 1974, and more wading birds bred there in each subsequent year. Shooters also hosted the earliest nesting activity of all the islands in the harbor, possibly because of the numerous tide pools trapped by piles of harbor drift and some 150 derelict vessels that were conducive to catching fish. Wading bird pairs at Shooters peaked at about four hundred in the mid-1990s after receiving a boost from the many individuals that deserted Pralls Island and Isle of Meadows following nearby oil spills. But the number dropped to 270 pairs in 1997, and then zero in 1998. Kerlinger believes the harbor herons deserted Shooters because of increased human activity on the island, primarily an illegal but regular encampment in the woods that made the birds nervous. But he also acknowledges that the rapid passage of foliage through different successional stages on the harbor islands may encourage population shifts in a kind of "dynamic equilibrium."

As we motor away from Shooters Island, Kerlinger hands me binoculars and tells me to look at the top of the skeletons of some abandoned drydocks, a pair of thirty-foot-high platforms. Completely ringed by nests of double-crested cormorants, they are a perfect fortress for the fish-eating birds that have rebounded strongly since the DDT pesticide era, not having been known to breed in New York Harbor until eight years ago. Some of these cormorant colonies are huge—about 850 on South Brother Island in

Nesting cormorant, South Brother Island, East River. (Ben Longstreth, Baykeeper)

the East River alone. But others are quite small; nine pairs, for instance, nest on the two little trees next to the peace arch sculpture on tiny U Thant Island across from the United Nations building.

Next stop is Pralls Island, a narrow slice of lowland parallel with the Staten Island shore. Before we land I notice strings of buoys set offshore of the island. Kerlinger says they are markers for crab pots. And in keeping with the largely uncoordinated natural resources regulations between the states, commercial harvest of blue crabs is entirely legal on the New York side of the channel, but is verboten one hundred yards away on the New Jersey side. Bird life is scarce that day on Pralls Island, but I am charmed to find a British soldier—a lichen with a bright red hat.

We also see washed-up horseshoe crab remains. At first glance, the army-tank-like horseshoe crabs of the harbor do not look like a source of food for diminutive shorebirds. But horseshoe crabs lay their eggs at the high-water mark on the extreme tides of full or new moons in May and June. The eggs are a major dietary boost for birds migrating from Central and South America in spring, especially at the crabs' region of maximum abundance, Delaware Bay. However, New York Harbor does not lack for the armored ones, and in places such as Jamaica Bay horseshoe crab eggs attract red knots, sanderlings, ruddy turnstones, and about twenty other shorebirds, plus laughing gulls, glossy ibis, and Canada geese. Snowy egrets eat the fish that swarm around horseshoe crab eggs.

Our final survey for the morning occurs on Isle of Meadows, a little farther south down the Arthur Kill. Bird activity is greater here, partly because it borders the Fresh Kills landfill and its enormous gull population. Kerlinger points out gull nests in a dry meadow area. Given how ubiquitous herring gulls are, it is difficult to believe that they originally nested only north and east of Portland, Maine. Once somewhat rare around New York, the four common gulls of the region may now total more than one million. And in colonizing the harbor they have not only adapted to unnatural food sources such as refuse but also learned to nest in new habitats, including salt marshes and human-altered areas. Adaptation appears to be part of gulls' arsenal; they are known to construct dummy nests to test the suitability of potential nest sites.

We also spot two kinds of warblers and a marsh hawk that glides quietly out of some nearby brush. Kerlinger shows me a glen used by the nesting herons. Twig nests are everywhere in the scrubbish trees, and it is easy to imagine the raucous din and feathery commotion at the little heron hamlet as the big birds fly in and out, feeding their young. At that time Kerlinger and several volunteers count the chicks, using a truck's rearview mirror mounted on a pole to peer into the nests as the parent birds scream bloody murder.

Although the harbor's suite of wading birds share nesting sites, they minimize competition by specializing in their feeding habits. The competitive exclusion principle states that when similar species compete for the same resources, one wins and the others go on to extinction. But the harbor herons have carved their own, albeit overlapping, niches by relying on differences in time of day, tidal levels, salinities, favored prey, and depth of water stalked to separate them. Black-crowned night-herons are generalists but are active at night; yellow-crowned night-herons favor fiddler crabs. Great and snowy egrets are mainly fish eaters, but great egrets do about equally well in fresh water and estuaries, whereas snowy egrets are more successful in fresh water. Glossy ibis concentrate on marsh snails, locating them tactilely with their bills rather than by sight. Cattle egrets did not even occur in North America until about fifty years ago, following what is believed to be a natural colonization of South America in 1880 from their native Africa, with subsequent spread throughout the New World. In Africa cattle egrets walk behind wildebeests and feed on insects kicked up by their hooves; in the United States, when they are not following lawn mowers and plows, they prey on frogs and insects.

The harbor herons, although thriving once again, feel the environmental stresses of the harbor. Two ornithologists, Drs. Alan Maccarone and John Brzorad, studied the effects on the birds of two major oil spills that occurred early in 1990 by comparing their observations from summer 1990 to those made in 1986 and 1987. Not surprising was their finding that the size of shrimp and small-fish populations of the Arthur Kill declined, or that the harbor herons responded by favoring more distant but unaffected freshwater sites for feeding. What wasn't expected, though, was that when Maccarone and Brzorad repeated the study seven years later, behavioral changes would still be evident.

10

New York Harbor retains a suprisingly original fauna—the Ellis Island receptiveness toward immigrants does not hold for new nonhuman species. All around the world organisms are by accident being exchanged among water bodies, usually having been carried unwittingly by oceangoing ships. These ships pick up ballast water in one port and then discharge it in another, often introducing the eggs or larvae of animals that take a liking to their new surroundings. In earlier centuries wooden vessels visiting the harbor carried rocks as ballast; these most likely included organisms that could have survived long journeys in damp holds. Later the rocks may have been dumped overboard or used as landfill, liberating the invaders to try foreign waters. The vessels themselves carried fouling and boring organisms. Because transatlantic commerce preceded marine science in New York Harbor and New England, it may be that some of the species scientists assume are native to both shores of the Atlantic were actually carried to the western Atlantic through exploration or trade.

Some ports, such as San Francisco's, appear to be under siege by exotic life forms that are claiming ecological niches only tenuously held by its depauperate native flora and fauna—in recent years new plants and animals have been discovered there at a rate of one every fourteen weeks. And while these new species may increase local biodiversity, something of a holy grail among ecologists, all but a few nonnatives to North America such as brown trout and peacock bass have been deemed detrimental, representing a kind of flip side to otherwise desirable biodiversity.

76

The fresh waters of the Hudson River have sustained a high rate of invasion—an estimated one new species (including plants) per year since 1840. But New York Harbor has either been the recipient of fewer invasives or is more immune to exotic creatures (one study in the United Kingdom found that only about 10 percent of attempted colonizations become established). The list of aquatic colonizers of any consequence to New York Harbor and surrounding waters is short: the European periwinkle (appearing first in Nova Scotia in 1840), the Asian seaweed *Codium fragile* (dead man's fingers), various sea squirts, the shipworm *Teredo navalis*, and the green crab. Just north of the harbor, in the brackish waters of the lower Hudson, a small bivalve abounds, the southern marsh clam *Rangia* (native to the Gulf of Mexico); it overlaps slightly in distribution with the more salt-shy zebra mussel. In 1994 Cathy Drew caught a pair of unfamiliar crabs with red eyes and purplish shells, and stored them dry in her desk drawer for future reference. Some time later a friend noticed them and told her they were Japanese shore crabs, a recent invader of the mid-Atlantic coast, first noticed at Cape May, New Jersey, in 1988. Drew has since found them under Pier 26 in large numbers, where they appear to have displaced the indigenous mud crabs.

Zebra mussels are attractive little striped bivalves native to the fresh waters of eastern Europe; they entered North America dramatically via bilgewater in the late 1980s. The first ones were noticed in Lake Erie in 1988, but they had exploded across all five Great Lakes by 1990, in quantities such that they clogged power-plant intakes. The first zebra mussels noticed in the Hudson River were found in 1991, near Catskill, New York. But by 1992 they had spread across the entire freshwater tidal Hudson, encrusting any hard bottom available in densities of 17,000 per square meter and reaching an absurdly huge total population estimated at 550 billion individuals. All the zebra mussels in North America also benefited in a curious way from their trip to the New World—they don't appear to have any of the parasites that typically afflict native European populations. Having been carried as eggs or larvae, they simply didn't host the parasites that infect adult zebra mussels. (This provides the luxury of selectively introducing parasites to help control zebra mussels. Still, this is always a risky endeavor because no one knows for sure which other organisms the parasites might infect.) Zebra mussels in the Hudson now extend southward to below Peekskill, their numbers dwindling at salinities of about five parts per thousand (about thirty parts per thousand less than full-strength seawater). Although stopping just shy of the harbor, zebra mussels affect the fresh water that flows into it. Since 1992 researchers have found a consistent summertime oxygen depletion of about 20 percent that appears to be the result of those half-zillion mussels respiring.

The zebra mussels are influencing waters whose food chain from the bottom up was already somewhat unusual. In "classical" estuaries phytoplankton and rooted plants harness sunlight and consume nutrients, providing food for zooplankton and higher levels. But the Hudson River receives vast amounts of organic and inorganic matter as runoff from its watershed, and this results in a turbid river with poor light penetration. This very un-Caribbean-like water makes life more difficult for phytoplankton; they can capture sunlight only when the river's currents cause them to rise near the surface, but they must burn their own energy to continue living in darkness. In shallow parts of the river photosynthesis by phytoplankton is roughly equal to their own respiration—they harness as much energy as they burn. In deep sections, however, respiration may be five times higher as individual algal cells drift around the mid- and bottom depths and receive only brief exposures to sunlight. The net result is a link in the food chain that uses up more energy than it produces and an oxygen deficit for the fresh waters that flow downstream to the harbor.

Zebra mussels filter the water at extraordinary rates, each molecule of H_2O passing through a bivalve every two to three days instead of every fifty days (as was the case prior to their colonization), and they have cropped the numbers of phytoplankton in the river by some 85 percent. Two major ecological changes that might have been expected as a consequence of the phytoplankton reduction have failed to happen. One is a pronounced clarification of the Hudson, as occurred in Lake Erie and the St. Lawrence River after zebra mussels combed out much of their algae. But because most of its turbidity is caused by inorganic material that can't be consumed, the Hudson, to the disappointment of many, has become only slightly more transparent. The other potential change was a crash of the fish populations that would have been expected to rely on phytoplankton to feed their larvae. Again, because the Hudson has so much detritus in it from its watershed, the major foundation for its food chain is bacteria, not phytoplankton, and fish seem to be coping as well as ever.

3

THE MEDIUM

Sewers, Sludge, and Other
Forms of Water Torture

"Now some people think that they're pretty damned clever,
They think once they flush it it's gone forever;
But they'd better remember where the sewers all meet,
The next time they ask for an oyster to eat. Oh ..."

Keith Sullivan
"You Can't Eat the Oysters"

1

IN 1939 CARL CARMER WROTE: "The Hudson of the people's dream is a river of clear water." If only a dream, it must have been a recurring one, fueled by its then-nightmarish qualities. Few water bodies have received the variety and volume of noxious wastes as have the Hudson River and New York Harbor. In the early 1900s the Metropolitan Sewerage Commission of New York reported gross sewage pollution as far as fifteen miles from Manhattan; in 1906 "seas of floating garbage were described."

81

Exterior of a free-floating bath house on New York Harbor.

Floating baths rimmed Manhattan but were plagued by sewage; at the East Ninety-sixth Street bath there were "swimming children with masses of filth collected on their head and shoulders." People caught typhoid fever merely from handling oyster and clamshells.

Beyond drifting trash and simple sewage is the speciose world of chemical pollution. The dioxin of Newark Bay is only one spirit in a potent boilermaker that includes three hundred thousand pounds of PCBs from the upper Hudson's now-defunct General Electric plants and more from countless leaky transformers in landfills all the way south to New York City; the ubiquitous petroleum-based polynuclear aromatic hydrocarbons, or PAHs, such as benzene and toluene; and arsenic, copper, mercury, and lead—the heavy metals of industry and gasoline combustion. PCBs now permeate the entire estuary. Some of the highest concentrations of heavy metals in the world are found in the Arthur Kill. A little

Interior of bath house. Particles of floating sewage were often visible.
(Metropolitan Sewerage Commission of New York)

south of Lady Liberty the garish Port Liberté development in
Jersey City rises Oz-like on a chromium-waste landfill. Although
Rachel Carson's *Silent Spring* was published in 1962, it took nearly
a decade before DDT was banned, and traces of the pesticide are
still detected around the harbor. During World War I and shortly
thereafter patches of floating oil ignited in various sections of New
York Harbor, which helped lead to passage of the Federal Oil
Pollution Act of 1924. In his journal Robert Juet recorded that
Henry Hudson's men were pleased by the grass and flowers on the
New Jersey side of the Hudson "and very sweet smells came from
them." But for much of this century the tank-rimmed shore of New
Jersey's Bayonne Peninsula has been known as the "chemical coast."

To the harbor's toxic amalgamation was added staggering
quantities of raw sewage—by 1910 six hundred million gallons per
day of untreated waste was being discharged from New York City

83

alone. This undigested organic matter overfertilized the water column while screaming for oxygen in its rush toward decomposition. The resultant "biological oxygen demand," accelerated in the warmth of summer, depleted oxygen to less than two parts per million, the minimum level tolerable for many organisms. Underwater deserts ensued—fish swam off and sessile creatures perished. Throughout a large portion of the harbor a pattern of marginally habitable waters during colder months and oxygen-starved waters during warm periods lasted for much of this century.

The scope of the problem of human waste across the entire harbor can be appreciated by the population changes in Manhattan alone. The census of 1656 revealed 120 houses and one thousand occupants, by 1698 the number of people was only five times greater, and in 1790 it numbered thirty-three thousand. But about one hundred years later, in 1900, there were more than two million residents of Manhattan exercising their daily physiological imperative. The overall New York City population has hovered around eight million from 1935 to the present, and that does not include the suburbs. It results in an extraordinary amount of fecal matter to be dealt with—most conveniently by release into a water body. It's been said that if New York City had been located where Albany is at the head of the tidal Hudson, the wastes would have overwhelmed the river and the Hudson would have perished a long time ago. Fortunately, the harbor's connections to the ocean and Long Island Sound have diluted these wastes, resulting in sickness but not death.

But New York Harbor did reach a critical condition because of sewage. The original sewerage system dates from the introduction of drinking water from the Croton River to New York City in 1840, but that sewage was discharged untreated into harbor

Sewer outlet, Jersey City, c. 1909. (Metropolitan Sewerage Commission of New York)

waters. Supervision of the system was placed under the control of the city government by 1850, and in 1865 a general sewerage scheme to serve the whole city was adopted. A corollary was that piers should be built with "open pilings," with spaces in between rather than rock-filled cribs so as to allow wastes to wash down the rivers. (These open pilings also allowed "dock rats" to flourish; not vermin, but petty thieves who preyed on ships tied to the docks. They often operated from rowboats and escaped through the open pilings. Some built "dens" under the wharves where they could hide, and even cook.) The first wastewater treatment plant in the region was built at Coney Island in 1886, a crude facility designed to capture floating material. But in 1914 sewage pollution caused New York City to begin closing its public beaches, including those in Manhattan and Brooklyn (except Coney Island), in the Bronx as far as Clason Point, in Queens, and on Staten Island from Fort Wadsworth to the Kill Van Kull and all of the Arthur Kill.

Pollution was recognized as a serious problem in 1903 by the creation of the New York Bay Pollution Commission, which soon became the Metropolitan Sewerage Commission. This body conducted a comprehensive survey of the harbor's condition between 1906 and 1914, at a time when the booming population was sending an onslaught of raw sewage to the region's waters. The results of the study, commonplace for an urbanized system at that time, are stupefying by today's environmental standards and perhaps need to be exhumed if we are to fully appreciate how much the harbor has improved since then. Much of the bottom was covered with sludge: black in color from sulfide of iron; oxygenless; its fermentation generating carbonic acid and ammonia waste; and putrefying continuously, giving off bubbles of methane gas, so actively in some places "that the water takes on the appearance of effervescence accompanied by a sound like rain falling upon the water." Water-quality goals were not lofty. The report went on to calculate approximately what sewage-to-harbor-water ratios could be reached to maintain oxygen levels at barely habitable levels for fish. The answer: a stout one part sewage to twenty parts water.

Concerning the sludge's distribution, "Practically the whole of the bottom of Upper New York Bay is covered with black, ill-smelling mud in which particles of sewage origin are distinguishable. In places these deposits have been found to attain a depth of over ten feet."

New York City has documented this ecological strangulation of its harbor with one of the most thorough and long-term municipal water-quality surveys performed anywhere. There is no universal indicator of water quality, but New York City's annual Harbor Survey Program tracks the basics at fifty-three stations: coliform bacteria from human wastes, dissolved oxygen, nutrients, the plant pigment chlorophyll, clarity, and more than a half-dozen other informative parameters. Begun in 1909, the survey showed abysmally low dissolved-oxygen levels in the lower Hudson River through 1960, when some improvement occurred because of upgrades to the Yonkers sewage plant. The turning point was the passage in 1972 of the Clean Water Act—a landmark miracle of legislation that required all the water bodies of the nation to be fishable and swimmable by 1985, with all discharges of pollutants eliminated. It took some time for the situation to reverse—a bit like turning an ocean liner around—but by the 1990s dissolved-oxygen levels had roughly doubled from their midcentury nadir.

Wanting to see a modern sewage-treatment facility, I show up at the North River plant off West 145th Street in Manhattan on the regular open-house tour day and find I am the only visitor, except for two college students who come and go quickly, allowing themselves fifteen minutes for the two-hour experience. Kiah Miller provides me with a personal lecture, a video presentation, and a walk through the mammoth structure. Two threads dominate—

the sheer scale of the enterprise, and how despite some 150 million gallons of sewage from more than six hundred thousand people working its way through the machinery each day, every square
foot of it appears completely sanitary. An odor is noticeable, but
it's faint and almost sweet, partly because Manhattan's sewer lines
are short and don't allow much time for feces to decay. Moreover,
having been added to the west side of Harlem in the 1980s in the
post–Robert Moses era when communities did not accept major
changes without complaint—if not fierce resistance—all-out
efforts have been made to control odors. Rooms within the plant
are pressurized; escaping air is captured, scrubbed in a two-stage
process, and then vented from smokestacks that rise high above
the state park lavishly furnished with recreational amenities that
sits on its roof. And the public is ready to sniff for problems. A
community odor panel was formed and trained as to the particular
smells that could emanate from the plant. When odors become a
nuisance, plant managers can zero in on the source based on the
panel's educated perceptions.

Sewage treatment has come a long way from the days when
Manhattan simply wore human wastes like a dirty diaper on the
surrounding harbor bottom. The sewage enters the plant well
below sea level and is first graded to remove solids, a simple
process called primary treatment. We peer down a screening
chamber and I ask Miller if they ever find diamond rings. He says,
"No, but we have caught fetuses, a live turtle that was taken home
as a pet, and large sums of money that we assume were flushed
during drug busts." The sewage then enters the primary settling
tanks for an average stay of one to two hours, after which most of
the sludge is removed. The remaining liquid begins secondary
treatment, which includes additional settling and aeration to stim-

ulate bacteria and other microbes to break down pollutants. The separated water is disinfected and released to the harbor in a state that technically is cleaner than the receiving waters. Much of the treatment process occurs in a room so huge and open to the air that it has its own weather—sometimes fog rises off the sewage raceways, collects on the ceiling, and rains onto the floor.

For six decades sewage sludge was shipped to a dump site just twelve miles out in the bight. The foul goo was released while the specialized vessels were moving, turning the foam in the boat's wake from white to jet black. This suffocated and noxious sixteen-square-mile zone was long known as our "Dead Sea." Dead, but not necessarily benign. Late in 1977, a loud but unexplained blast was heard over the metropolitan area. A theory that methane gas had belched upward from the sewage dump site and then was ignited by lightning was taken seriously until the air force admitted the sound's cause was a sonic boom from one of its jets, magnified by a temperature inversion. Sludge dumping was moved much farther offshore in 1987, to the "106-mile site" at the edge of the continental shelf. All ocean sludge dumping was halted in 1991. But this means that the unceasing stream has to be disposed of on land.

Today the sludge, following primary treatment, goes through simple but exhaustive processing—it is further dewatered and digested, which includes heating in special tanks without oxygen for fifteen to twenty days. There it even helps pay its way—the methane gas that fizzles out of it is trapped and used to run the plant's engines, providing one-third of its energy needs. In the end the sludge's volume is reduced by nine-tenths and it resembles moist clay. This highly rendered fecal matter is also not without value. Most of it is pelletized and converted to fertilizer by a private contractor, then sold to farmers around the country. Thus, when residents of the West Side of Manhattan buy produce in Gristedes or Fairway, they may be enjoying the fruits of their own wastes. And the North River plant is only one of fourteen similar sewage-treatment facilities in New York City. I walk away awestruck at the contrast between accounts of the harbor bottom smothered in raw bubbling sludge one hundred years earlier and a procedure today that slowly manipulates and reduces human wastes to a commodity.

2

Although the normal rush of sewage to the harbor is generally controlled by a serpentine collection network that ends with secondary treatment, the system falls apart during rain events when the capacity is exceeded, the tripping point being about twice the normal flow volume of dry periods. Then, street runoff combines with sewage to overwhelm treatment plants, the excess pouring untreated into the harbor from combined sewer overflows, called CSOs for short. When I worked in 1983 on Manhattan's Upper East Side, I'd take lunch breaks along the East River; after a downpour I'd watch streams of turds shoot by. CSOs are also the largest single source of pathogens and floating trash. The approximately 730 CSOs around the harbor are the nagging breaches in the overall reining-in and dehorning of sewage inputs. When Adam Brown dives following pronounced rainy periods, he sees dying and decaying sea life on structures downstream of CSOs. There are no easy solutions to the CSO problem. Ideally, street runoff and sewage should be separated, but the ill-devised system that combines them for about forty-five hundred of New York City's sixty-three hundred miles of sewers already is in place. The only reasonable alternative is beginning to be acted on where possible—the building of great storage tanks, ranging between seven million and thirty million gallons' capacity, to contain the combined rainwater and sewage runoff until it can be rerouted through treatment plants.

But as the sewage problem slowly improves another, more nebulous oxygen robber has come into focus. Nitrogen is the engine of coastal eutrophication, the nutrient enrichment that causes algae blooms, followed by algal decay and, subsequently, a drain on oxygen. As point sources of nitrogen have been tamed, more of the nitrogen entering the Hudson River and New York Harbor is coming from overhead—diffuse, unseen, but very real atmospheric fallout. Nitrogen climbs into the atmosphere as nitrogen oxides from gasoline and oil combustion and as ammonia from manure and fertilizer. This falls back to earth with rain and snow in the Hudson Valley and New York metropolitan area, eventually upsetting the harbor's nutrient balance.

The toxic medium that has enveloped the harbor's fish has affected them in various ways. Between 1967 and 1971 almost two dozen kinds of fish from the New York Bight were found to have fin rot. And at high levels for some species: more than 20 percent of bluefish, 16 percent of fluke, and 11 percent of weakfish. Fin rot is a progressive disease that includes lesions and ulcerated and eroding fin margins. Sometimes the skin is destroyed first, leaving the fin's rays and spines as naked stumps. I once caught two striped bass in a trawl net near the Statue of Liberty that lacked their pectoral, pelvic, and caudal fins; like lepers, they came out of the water together, but alone. The incidence of fin rot has gone down since then but today, a little farther up the Hudson, a noticeable percentage of white catfish are blind, their eyes covered with anomalous tissue growths.

Another peculiar response to this polluted estuary is shown by the Atlantic tomcod. The tomcod is a small inshore version of the commercially harvested codfish of the offshore banks; tomcod are bottom feeders sought by shorebound anglers all around the harbor. In the late 1970s scientists noticed that most Hudson River estuary tomcod had curious dark-colored spots on their livers. Further study showed that they were neoplastic hepatic lesions— liver cancer in plain English. And at extraordinary levels for a wild vertebrate population. A survey conducted in 1984 showed that almost half of the age-one tomcod and more than 90 percent of age-two specimens had cancerous or precancerous growths in their livers, compared to less than 10 percent in a control population from a relatively unpolluted estuary in Connecticut. Recent research puts most of the blame on PAHs. What may have saved the tomcod of the Hudson River from extinction is that they mature at the end of their first year, managing to reproduce before they succumb to cancer.

Although fish and shellfish may in the past have died because of a lack of oxygen or intense localized contamination, there is a rather common but sensational dying-fish phenomenon that is no more than a red herring as an ecological indicator. Often during warm weather, village halls or other government entities receive panicky calls about massive fish kills, as if some frightful chemical must be in the water. But the actors and the stage in this summer theater almost always turn out to be the same. Adult menhaden about one foot in length become corralled by hungry bluefish in a creek or some kind of cul-de-sac where the water is shallow, tepid, and holds less oxygen. As the terrified menhaden mill around tightly while under attack they defecate as part of the fright response, and their own respiration, along with the breakdown of their wastes, rapidly uses up available oxygen. Immense numbers of menhaden may perish this way, far more than are eaten by the bluefish, and they rot in place or drift elsewhere until they are picked up by a sanitation department or, more often, until decomposition does the job. And while it may be that reduced water quality has lowered the threshold for these events to occur, it is important to remember that Danckaerts described the same occurrence in a Staten Island creek in 1679.

Both the buildup of toxic contamination and its initial retreat have produced unexpected biological ironies. The explosion in numbers of striped bass in the Hudson River and the harbor is due partly to the 1975 discovery of unacceptable levels of PCBs in their flesh. The population was conserved through the inadvisibility of its consumption; because of contamination, commercial harvest of striped bass was curtailed in and around the Hudson River, and recreational harvest was sharply reduced. One estimate was that the Hudson's striper population grew in the 1980s about as fast as a decent investment—8 percent, compounded yearly. When the New York Yankees baseball team lost the 1997 playoffs to the Cleveland Indians, Mayor Rudolph Giuliani made good on a bet and sent the mayor of Cleveland ten pounds of striped bass caught in the East River. Perhaps this was Mayor Giuliani's quiet revenge: The New York State Health Department recommends eating only half a pound of locally harvested striped bass per month.

Also, for decades the harbor's malignant waters guarded the thousands of wooden pilings that hold up its piers against destruction by two very different forms of invasive invertebrates, grouped as the marine borers. Before the waters were fouled, timber piers and wharves were considered temporary, with an expected life of fourteen to seventeen years. The reputation of the harbor's dockage

Marine borer and ice damage to a Brooklyn pier. (Rob Gill, Port Authority of New York)

facilities varied across the decades, partly due to the borers. A visitor to New York shortly before the Revolution said, "I do not think there are any cities on this continent where the art of constructing wharves has been pushed to a further extent." But an editorial comment to *Scribner's Monthly* in 1872 stated, "We . . . can point to our docks as the dirtiest, the most insufficient, and the least substantial of any possessed by any first-class city on the face of the globe."

During the long era of protective pollution that followed, the chief threat to the docks was urine from the horses that pulled cargo on and off them; pilings lasted for many decades. Presently, as water quality improves, structures all over the harbor are succumbing to these underwater termites—in 1997 six people suddenly found themselves in the East River when part of a borer-damaged pier in Greenpoint gave way; two years earlier a portion of the woody underpinnings of FDR Drive collapsed.

Teredo—mollusks that can grow to six feet—dig deep mine shafts into timbers with their shells, which have evolved into tiny paired drill bits. The second form—*Limnoria*, little shrimplike creatures called gribbles—are more like strip miners, creating a mosaic pattern of burrows just under the surface of pilings. As they progress, auxiliary openings to the surface are made to allow water exchange for respiration, resulting in a honeycombed appearance. Pilings may develop an hourglass shape, with the less attacked sections above the mean high-water mark and below the mud line remaining substantially broader than the intervening zone, which may lose two inches of diameter annually. An assortment of fungi, including white rot, brown rot, and soft rot, may prep the wood prior to *Teredo* and *Limnoria* infestation.

Various concoctions have been brewed to stave borer damage. In the 1800s ship hulls were covered with a mix of "pitch and tar with essence of tobacco" or "rubbed with bacon and lime, or sandarac or oil." Later formulations included tar and felt with zinc sheathing; powdered glass in tar; and, more recently, creosote treated with copper, chrome, and arsenate. But having divers wrap pilings with plastic sheeting may be the most effective way to stem further marine borer damage. New options for construction materials also are being sought. The Tiffany Street Pier in the South Bronx, built in 1996 with a million and a half recycled soda bottles, was abandoned not long after it was built when one-third of it melted after being struck by lightning. Although ultrasound approaches to detect the presence of *Teredo* have been attempted, the uneven resonance of wood fibers makes these unreliable—only destructive sampling of the pilings using at least two-inch-diameter bored cores yields results that can be trusted. The scope of the marine borer menace to the harbor's sunken forests is massive— one study of two city piers in 1990 showed almost no *Teredo*, but by 1997 the animals were found in 95 percent of the core samples. The New York City Department of Transportation recently awarded a research and engineering contract to protect twelve of its piers, together composed of more than eight thousand timbers.

3

Each year seventeen hundred tankers carry eighteen billion gallons of petroleum to New York Harbor. A not inconsiderable amount of this finds its way into the water. The true crisis came in 1990. During its first six months more than one hundred spills and mishaps discharged over one million gallons of oil into the Arthur Kill and Kill Van Kull. The wildlife of the Arthur Kill greeted the new year assaulted by the largest of these releases, which lasted until January 2, when an Exxon pipeline ruptured and leaked 567,000 gallons of No. 2 fuel oil. The cleanup effort included sixty thousand feet of boom, 680 people, seventy vessels, forty vacuum trucks, and ten skimmers, but still only recovered about one-quarter of the spill. The remaining oil created a slick that poisoned the salt marshes around the breeding islands for the harbor herons and killed at least 650 ducks, geese, and gulls, twenty-eight muskrats, innumerable invertebrates, and broad stands of spartina. This was followed about two months later by an explosion on the Citgo Petroleum Corporation's barge *Cibro Savannah* that resulted in another 127,000 gallons of No. 2 heating oil coating the kills. On June 7 the tanker *BT Nautilus* ran aground and spilled 260,000 gallons of No. 6 oil near the Bayonne Bridge on the Kill Van Kull.

There was a bright side to the Exxon spill. The company's immediate response had been to play down its environmental consequences, claiming that if a spill had to occur somewhere in the harbor, the already severely degraded Arthur Kill was the best place. But several environmental groups quickly called attention to the harbor herons and other vibrant biological features of the Arthur Kill and, together with federal and state agencies, negotiated a settlement with the oil company. By 1991 Exxon had paid fifteen million dollars in damage and penalty costs, of which eleven million was earmarked for restoration, land acquisition, and environmental studies of the Arthur Kill.

Oil spills may be accidental, but the inner portion of the New York Bight has long been an all-too-convenient place to dispose purposefully of that which is unwanted. As recently as 1934 garbage was dumped off scows at the entrance to the harbor. The Tin Can Grounds, today a popular fishing spot just outside the Lower New York Bay, was an early grave for household trash; the Subway Grounds are made of debris blasted in the construction of the Eighth Avenue subway tunnels; and the Seagull Grounds were

Garbage scows being loaded for dumping at sea. (*Seaport* magazine)

named after the hungry seabirds that would hover over the organic refuse jettisoned there. Farther out were the Acid Grounds, an area of water stained yellow from sulfuric acid–acid sulfate wastes dumped by barge from a New Jersey titanium plant; the dyed waters proved curiously attractive to bluefish. (Other popular fishing grounds in the New York Bight were named for events in the years they were discovered: the Cholera Banks during the 1832 epidemic, and the Klondike Banks during the Klondike gold rush.)

Much of the garbage dumped at sea drifted back to shore in fields that were acres across; items from the dumping ground washed up fifty miles to the east at Smith Point, Long Island, and seventy-five miles to the south at Atlantic City, New Jersey. And justice was served—some even made it back into the Upper New York Bay. Often driftwood would mix in oily slicks called "sleek."

Unloading rubbish at sea near Sandy Hook, c. 1896. In 1896, more than 760,000 cubic yards were disposed of in this manner.

Where it accumulated near shore, the wood was collected by Manhattan residents for their stoves; sometimes covered with an inch of grease, it presumably burned well. In 1906 the Metropolitan Sewerage Commission of New York studied the problem by posting observers or having lifeguards track the detritus they had to clean off the ocean beaches. The Long Beach, Long Island, report for July included: two dead cats, several dead rats, decayed vegetables, fifteen to twenty crates of good lemons, pieces of fat meat and bread, a dead fowl, a mattress and bed, tin cans, bottles, paper, and horse dung. One woman at Bradley Beach, New Jersey, left hastily after swimming into the corpse of a dog.

Household trash has long been discarded in landfills created in wetlands around the harbor's edge, typically low-lying marshy areas that were drastically underappreciated for their ecological value

Gathering driftwood for fuel at the Battery, c. 1909. (Metropolitan Sewerage Commission of New York)

when dumping began. The three-thousand-acre Fresh Kills landfill on the shores of the Arthur Kill was inaugurated in 1948, and a steady torrent of New York City's refuse has resulted in a mound as high as a seventeen-story building and three and a half times the area of Central Park and visible to orbiting astronauts. Every day except Sunday another fourteen thousand tons are added. Started at a time when environmental controls were almost unheard of, the challenge now is in shutting it down by the target date of 2001, when every aspect of its existence must meet stern environmental standards originally unplanned for. Fresh Kills is the last of the city's dozens of landfills and incinerators to be closed, and its neighbors cannot wait. The dump is essentially one endless fart, passing some thirty million cubic feet of garbage gas, including methane, into the air per day. Another ten million cubic feet already heats fourteen thousand Staten Island homes.

Coney Island bathers' reactions to floating trash. (*Seaport* magazine)

The major hazard to the harbor from Fresh Kills is the rainwater that percolates through the trash, picking up contaminants and moving laterally out of the landfill. To corral this polluted stream, the city has constructed a complex system of cutoff walls, drains, and pumps, and a treatment plant that handles 1.4 million gallons per day. Two of four sections are now permanently closed, with an impermeable membrane as their final cover.

What will become of Fresh Kills when it is closed down remains to be seen. Some old, low-elevation New York City landfills, such as Great Kills on Staten Island, that were built on marshes are now parks. Typically, tall modern landfills are topped with a thin layer of soil and planted with only grasses to prevent erosion; the engineers fear that the roots of trees could potentially invade through the clay caps and geotextile liners normally used to rein in the bad stuff. But the end result is often a quilt of sparse weeds and reeds of low ecological value, without the usual successional stages of flora culminating in forest. If Marc Matsil, the director of the Natural Resources Group of the New York City Department of Parks, has his way, though, based on experiments in England, New York's first mountain will be planted with a ready-made oak-hickory forest, creating a little piece of the Appalachians by the sea.

One of the preoccupations of harbor managers is controlling trash that is dumped or blows into the water and then drifts around, gathering in wind slicks or tide rips or washing up on beaches. For something so common, resource agencies have adopted a curious term—*floatables*, as if this is only a hypothetical concern and not something one sees simply by viewing the water. Far-from-hypothetical floating rubbish received enormous publicity in 1988 when medical wastes including syringes, along with crack vials and dead rats, washed up on New York beaches. Much of it was traced back to the Fresh Kills landfill.

4

If you really wish to know what floats around New York Harbor, consult the many electric-generating stations that use harbor water to cool their generators. These intakes must filter the water, at least coarsely, before passing it through their systems. As a series of continuous operating mechanized strainers, they present an excellent window on the life and drift of the harbor.

"Don't you have something better to do with your time?" says a worker at the Consolidated Edison station at East Fourteenth Street on the East River, incredulous that I've actually come to see the garbage-catching operation. I meet some of the engineers and am issued a hard hat; we walk through a world of pipes and hardware in a tunnel under FDR Drive and emerge alongside the river by the water intake, first passing by a barge busy with workers retrofitting the bulkhead against *Teredo* worms.

Inside a squat building are banks of enclosed, rotating "traveling screens" with water jets that wash animals and detritus back into the river. A worker opens a port for me to look inside, and I am sprayed with water that bears little resemblance to Perrier. There isn't much to see because there isn't much trash in the river at this moment. But the larger screens racked on shore are covered with streamers of plastic sheeting, maybe the most pervasive garbage of the harbor. In a yearlong study of the plant an appalling 3,687 gallons of plastic and paper were recorded. Aquatic vegetation (3,443 gallons) and terrestrial vegetation (2,540 gallons) were not far behind.

Then there are the animals. Two groups of invertebrates, bryozoans and tunicates, added up to almost 13,415 gallons.

Dead whale being towed down the Kill Van Kull. (Helena Andreyko, Hudson River Foundation)

Ctenophores, jellyfishlike ovals that light up at night, were absent in winter but made up 2,228 gallons of mush in July alone. Likewise, no blue claw crabs were ensnared between January and April, but more than a thousand individuals per month showed up on the screens in October and November. Fish, too, are well represented. Bay anchovies were pulled into the plant at an extraordinary rate, an estimated 227,489 specimens in one year—equal alone to the total number of individuals of the other sixty-six species also enumerated over the same period.

Some of the creatures that drift around New York Harbor could choke a power plant. One blustery October day I'm part of a group hosting three Ukrainian fish biologists for a tour of the harbor. The Ukrainians listen courteously as we tell them about its various environmental problems, but it's clear they are most excited by its visual aspects—the view of Manhattan from the water and, most of all, the Statue of Liberty. The sights remain the standard ones until we are passing down the Kill Van Kull and our captain shouts, "That ship is towing a whale!" She spins our boat around and we pull alongside the *Driftmaster*, the Army Corps of Engineers' blocky vessel dedicated to clearing the waters of debris that is hazardous to navigation, including dead whales. We pass downwind and immediately find that the whale stinks. But what a sight! It's a fifty-one-foot-long fin whale found in a habitat completely unfit for outsized cetaceans—among the wharves of Port Newark. Surprisingly, though, such finds are not rare. Large ships whose bows have the modern profile that includes a concave curve and bulbous bottom sometimes pick up dead whales at sea, like big bugs on an automobile grille, the crews remaining unaware of their impromptu masthead until the ship halts and the whale floats to the surface.

5

The backwaters and commercial dead ends of New York Harbor all have parallel histories of transformation from almost paradisiacal creeks rich in fish and shellfish and lined with salt hay through descents into industrial infernos replete with environmental atrocities and then back again to some—often severely reduced—modicum of ecological functionality. Early in the nineteenth century the Passaic was considered the best fishing stream in New Jersey, producing great quantities of shad, sturgeon, and resident species. By 1894 it had become a cesspool. Acid fumes caused the paint on houses along the river to blister and peel. Homes were deserted because of the fumes and stench. In 1970 the Passaic River was listed as one of the ten most polluted rivers in the country. Researchers burned their hands taking samples of acidic black gunk oozing from drainpipes along the banks. The entire six-mile riverbed in Newark is a Superfund site. Red-tailed hawks are sometimes seen along the river, but only because they hunt the water rats. The *New York Times* reported that someone telephoned the Passaic River Coalition, an environmental group, saying he had a client who faced the death penalty in a murder trial. The lawyer said the man went swimming in Newark in the 1960s and wondered if something in the water could have caused neurological damage. The coalition's head speculated that his defense would be, "The river made me do it."

But there is hope for the Passaic River. A skipper tells his passengers to remove their life jackets in the middle of the Passaic in downtown Newark because they make better targets. "Crack heads with guns sometimes shoot at the little boats." Nonetheless he is out there, giving tours. Moreover, the Army Corps of Engineers has unveiled plans for a twenty-five-million-dollar pedestrian promenade curving along two miles of riverbank. This will block erosion, unite key pieces of urban renewal, and, most important for this corner of the harbor, bring the public to the water.

On the east side of New York Harbor there are two waterways, Newtown Creek and the Gowanus Canal, that have been punched senseless by man. Newtown Creek in Queens has received equivalent abuse but appears to receive less attention than the Gowanus these days, perhaps because its neighborhoods are less trendy. In colonial times large ships could sail four miles up Newtown Creek and into a large lagoon near Maspeth Heights; upstream was the two-hundred-acre Maspeth Marsh, fished and hunted in the early 1800s by aristocrats who owned summer homes along its shores.

Conditions in Newtown Creek were much worse by the late 1800s. Winds carried sludge acid fumes across residential neighborhoods of Queens, Brooklyn, and Manhattan's East Side, prompting families to shut their windows or, when circumstances became unbearable, to flee the city for several days. In summer 1881 *Harper's Weekly* ran a three-week series of exposés about the abominable conditions on Newtown Creek. These included dramatic descriptions of adults choking in their sleep, children growing pale, and babies dying in their mothers' arms from the stenches. In September 1891 members of the Fifteenth Ward Smelling Committee embarked on a voyage up the creek to determine the sources of foul odors that permeated their streets. The air became riper as they passed cargo ships, manure scows, a dog pound, and sausage factories where they saw heaps of flesh rotting in open doorways. When they reached the oil refineries "the stenches began asserting themselves with all the vigor of fully developed stenches." A map from 1896 lists "offensive trade establishments located on Newtown Creek, Borough of Queens, requiring permits from the Board of Health." Among these were the Barnett Starch Works, Acme Fertilizer Company, Nichols Chemical Works, U.S. & Canada Degreasing Syndicate, manure barges, and, not surprisingly off by itself, a suffocating combination—the night-soil boat and dead animal wharf.

The scale of industrial commerce on Newtown Creek in the early twentieth century can best be appreciated by comparing the amount of freight carried along its four miles to that of the more than one-thousand-mile-long Mississippi River. From 1915 through 1917, 5,500,000 tons of freight were hauled annually up and down America's heartland; 5,620,000 tons were shipped on this little tidal arm of the East River and at twice the total value. Newtown Creek also was New York's first concentrated oil-refining district. By 1872 John D. Rockefeller and Standard Oil had gained control of all but one of the distilleries, and by 1880 he had more than one hundred stills along the creek that each week consumed more than three million gallons of crude oil. Virtually every stage in the refining process created a waste-disposal problem. Estimates of the losses are astounding. If roughly 5 percent of the initial crude petroleum ended up as coke residue, gas, or other by-products, the Newtown Creek refineries would have produced about three hundred thousand gallons of waste per week.

Today Newtown Creek is far from healthy. All that spillage left behind enough oil that the creek is not only a depot but also a source. Pumps bring oil back up from recovery wells at the sites of the original refineries. And a system is in place to capture petroleum as it flows sideways toward the canal from an "oil field" under Greenpoint. The fish most highly contaminated with PCBs, chlordane, and dieldrin found in the 1993 New York Harbor toxics study were eels from Newtown Creek; their PCB values were as much as nine times the Federal Drug Administration's tolerance limit. Oxygen still reaches zero levels in its bottom waters during summer. My colleague Dennis Suszkowski, science director of the Hudson River Foundation, once visited the creek during warm weather and noticed strange umbrellalike structures. Someone told him they were "blop-blops"—sheets of sewage sludge that capture methane gas produced by rotting matter that then float to the surface like parachutes in reverse, leaving the top of the water decorated like bad 1960s pop art.

6

Then there is the Gowanus Canal. It's a sunny Sunday morning in late August when a friend, Rob Maass, and I join a crowd gathered on the Brooklyn waterfront at the Riverside Cafe. We have all signed up for an unlikely, somewhat perverse experience—a guided "postapocalyptic" tour of the Gowanus.

108

It is difficult to discuss the Gowanus Canal without using the term *legendary*, which evokes the notoriety this simple ditch has achieved for suffering centuries of pollution. This in turn has generated a morbid curiosity—not necessarily of the dauntless kind where one would explore the canal on one's own, but rather a cautious one where people would rubberneck at a massive environmental accident from the safety of a sleek tour boat. On an earlier tour one participant couldn't stay off his cellular phone because "I just had to tell everyone where I was; nobody would believe it"!

The surprisingly popular tours are led by the executive director of the Brooklyn Center for the Urban Environment, John Muir, a barrel-chested baritone who obviously relishes the role and who sports a captain's outfit on tour days. We slip down Buttermilk Channel and past Governors Island, where the Governor's House was built for the British head of the New York colony from taxes levied on people who wore pearl rings, slave owners, and bachelors over the age of twenty-five. Beyond the island we watch a parasailer being pulled around the harbor by boat—gaining a seagull's view—as Muir offers facts about the neighborhoods along the Brooklyn shore. Red Hook, for instance, noted for its reddish sediments, retains its appellation, but Yellow Hook, named for its yellowish sands, reminded too many of *yellow fever* and so is known today as Bay Ridge.

The Gowanus Canal itself follows the natural lay of Gowanus Creek—originally Gowane's Creek—lying in Gowane's Land, an area named for the leader of the Canarsee Indians who lived nearby. A swampy but fertile drainage, the creek supported great quantities of "Gowanus" oysters, Brooklyn's first export, said to be as large as dinner plates. Danckaerts stated in his journal that the Chesapeake oysters of Maryland and Virginia were good but that those from Gowanus Creek were better—in fact "the best in the country." Freeke's Mill and Yellow Mills dammed its headwaters in the late 1700s, and prints from as late as 1867 show schooners moored in pastoral vistas. But images don't reveal stenches; by 1880 residents up to a mile away complained, calling the canal "a repulsive repository of rank odors."

The canal bustled in the late nineteenth and first half of the twentieth centuries, becoming by World War I the busiest commercial canal in the United States. Much of the timber, sand, and brownstone that built modern Brooklyn passed through the Gowanus. There were foundries, slaughterhouses, cement makers, flour mills, gashouses, and other fouling enterprises along its banks. Dye works brightened its waters with the various colors of each day's production, lending the canal the nickname "Lavender Lake." Sailors and the requisite bars and rooming houses surrounded the area. And the poor people of the neighboring communities did not always heed the health threats the canal posed. Some mothers even carried their asthmatic children to the canal's bridges to inhale what they believed were health-giving vapors rising from its waters.

To enter the Gowanus Canal from its mouth today is to see the scars and scabs of its subsequent history strung and heaped along its banks. But the echoes of energy and industriousness are unmistakable, like closing time at a carnival on Saturday night. The Isbrandtsen shipping line pier, broken in midsection, kneels in the water as if exhausted. The Port Authority's Grain Terminal, which received midwestern wheat via the Great Lakes and Erie Canal, has moldered, unused for thirty years. Portable electric-generating stations owned by Consolidated Edison, once considered temporary, still hum, tucked into a backwater. A solid-waste transfer station handles streams of garbage loaded on barges. Oil depots occupy stretches that previously hosted depots for coal, the preceding fossil fuel of choice. Overhead, creeping trucks and cars rain soot from a bridge along the worst highway in America—the Gowanus Expressway, a road that is anything but. All that is left of one large warehouse-sized structure is its bones, steel girders twisted and bent artistically in a fire so as to extemporaneously form a stark-looking sculpture.

The canal narrows as we slip farther into Brooklyn. In fact encroachment from unregulated landfilling has resulted in a waterway that is officially one hundred feet wide but now actually measures about sixty feet across. The skipper keeps the vessel near the center of the canal to avoid the silt shoulders alongside the bulkheads; the Army Corps of Engineers halted regular dredging of the canal because it wasn't cost effective. Abu Moulta Ali, an environmental scientist on the Brooklyn Center's staff, takes a water sample. A test shows the oxygen level at 1.8 parts per million, a level below the comfort zone of most organisms and one that is less than half the value Ali obtained near the mouth of the canal earlier in the tour. Indeed, the Gowanus Canal is hardly a cradle of biodiversity; we see little sign of aquatic life, just a few silverside minnows skittering across the surface. But fishermen still try their luck near the canal's mouth. Recently, two anglers thought their luck was pretty good when they snagged a large suitcase they imagined contained bundles of cash. Upon opening it, there was no time for disappointment—only horror: It was filled with human body parts, and not all from one person. Without doubt the most noteworthy biological event within the canal's industrial history was the appearance of a large shark in 1950. Ali showed me a scrapbook about the canal that included a photograph of the shark from the *Brooklyn Daily Eagle*. Fittingly, it is a dismal

Shark being shot in Gowanus Canal, 1950. (*Brooklyn Daily Eagle*)

scene—policemen's bullets spray the water near the creature as hundreds of people watch along the bulkheads.

The Gowanus Canal's lack of oxygen is due to its stagnation as a dead-end ditch that has accumulated decades of sewage outfall, which fuels algae blooms that die off and use oxygen as they rot. Locals said you could flush your toilet, race down to the canal, and watch your own feces emerge. Joseph Mitchell wrote that sightseers would come to the Gowanus Canal to look at the black, bubbly water where the "rising and breaking of sludge bubbles makes the water seethe and spit." In the past this sewage also included cholera, hepatitis, and typhoid vectors. All of which complemented a stream of lead, cadmium, mercury, and petroleum runoff to create a stench that was the canal's most noteworthy characteristic. On the dry, breezy day of my tour the eau de Gowanus is palpable but not overpowering; however, there are those who say you don't truly know the canal if "you ain't never smelled that funk."

A true dead end with almost no natural circulation, Gowanus Canal was the harbor's appendix, an organic sink that grew more fetid through the decades until an artificial but effective engineering solution rinsed it out. On June 21, 1911, a young woman tossed carnations on the water in front of 350 dignitaries to inaugurate the flushing system, which included a twelve-foot-wide brick tunnel built perpendicular to the head of the canal from Buttermilk Channel near Governors Island under Degraw and Hoyt Streets. The tunnel was fitted with a bronze propeller salvaged from a ship and rigged to pump water in either direction, in concert with the tides. The apparatus worked well until the 1960s when the propeller shaft broke, supposedly because a worker dropped an access manhole cover into the pump chamber. The pump system wasn't fixed because city engineers concluded that a new sewage-treatment plant being built nearby at Red Hook would reduce the stench of the newly ponded canal.

But stagnation persisted despite overall improvements in water quality over the rest of the harbor. Finally, the simple wisdom of the original pumping system prevailed, and the machinery was repaired. The last stage before the blades began to spin was the clearing of two thousand tons of polluted mud from where the tunnel meets the canal so that this material wouldn't be driven into the harbor.

Because the Ninth Street Bridge isn't yielding to boat traffic this day, our tour makes it only halfway up the canal, missing some of its cul-de-sacs, which are said to be filling in and reverting to salt marsh. Wanting to see some of what we missed by boat, Maass and I drive to the head of the canal at the ancient, swiveling

Carroll Street Bridge. The funk here smells even funkier as a mysterious milky substance pours out of a drainpipe. But I realize this day that the Gowanus Canal is no longer déclassé. Not only has the *New York Times* just published a long article on the growing reverence for the canal, but there on the bridge are a photographer and gaggle of assistants shooting a fashion model against the backdrop of the glorious Gowanus.

4

THE VESSEL
Bank and Bottom, Bulldozers and Blasts

"There now is your insular city of the Manhattoes,
belted round by wharves as Indian isles
by coral reefs—commerce surrounds it with her surf."

Herman Melville
Moby-Dick (1851)

1

THE THRESHOLD OF WATER quality necessary to once again support a diversity of life in New York Harbor has been crossed. The real uncertainties concerning the future of the harbor surround its habitat—bank and bottom. The profile of the harbor today bears little resemblance to Henry Hudson's or Giovanni da Verrazano's descriptions. In 1524 Verrazano wrote presciently, but for the wrong reasons, that the land around the harbor "was not without some properties of value, since all the hills showed signs of minerals." (Verrazano's viewing of New York Harbor may have

115

been his high point in the New World; four years later he was murdered and cannibalized on a Caribbean island.)

A stream, almost certainly supporting brook trout, ran west to the Hudson near Forty-second Street, not far from where an Orvis shop now outfits customers for trout-fishing expeditions upstate. (Minetta Brook in Greenwich Village held trout until the late eighteenth century.) Manhattan was coursed by many other flowages, with names like Cedar Creek, Montayne's Rivulet, and Old Wreck Brook; all were eventually ignobled as underground sewers. The large, forty-foot-deep Collect Pond provided fresh water (one of its sources was named Tea-water Spring, reputed to offer the best drinking water in Manhattan) and good fishing where the Manhattan Criminal Court now stands; the world's first steamship was given a trial run there seven years before Fulton's *Clermont*. Broad Street covers a reed-lined inlet called the Graught; Beaver Street in the financial district is named after the rodents that built dams there. (Their predator, wolves, hung on in Fort Washington Heights until 1686.) The marsh replaced by Washington Square offered excellent duck hunting. A roaring gut known as Little Hell Gate divided the later-conjoined Randalls and Wards Islands and a smaller island, known as Sunken Meadow. U Thant Island did not exist. Coney Island was an island.

Almost every part of the harbor, including its 770 miles of waterfront, has since been bulkheaded, platformed, filled, drained, dredged, blasted, rerouted, tunneled, or bridged. Coal ash and refuse expanded Rikers Island sevenfold; Ellis Island is eight times larger than its original size. Canal Street rests on a former canal that had been dug through a marsh, the Lispenard Meadows. Filling of the shallows swelled lower Manhattan by one-third. Battery Park City is built on sand mined from the bottom of the harbor. Water Street now lies five hundred feet from the water. But much of this expansion was passive—ship ballast, dredge spoils, cinders, and trash were dumped between piers, some forty-foot slips shoaling to eight feet in only fifteen years. Dock owners simply built out farther, steadily reducing the width of the waterways to such a degree as to spawn the River and Harbor Act of 1888, which established today's pier-head lines.

Canals altered the shoreline. The Morris Canal, now a short dead end off the Hudson River, once allowed barges to deliver coal eastward and iron ore westward between Jersey City and the Lehigh Valley in Pennsylvania. And the Harlem River's pro-

Morris Canal today. (Virginia Rolston Parrott)

nounced bends were reduced to create the Harlem Ship Canal, leaving a piece of Manhattan attached to the Bronx—a division still recognized as Marble Hill, Manhattan.

Lafayette Island, former home to seventy-three-gun Fort Lafayette, is now the Brooklyn-side base of the Verrazano Narrows Bridge. Hoffman and Swinburne Islands, visible to the south from the bridge, were built from rubble as quarantine islands after Staten Island residents kept burning down their own quarantine hospitals because of their fear of yellow fever. The borough of Queens cannibalized the beach resort Tallman Island by landfilling; Brooklyn created Floyd Bennett Field by joining Barren Island with its mainland.

Although the natural maximum depth of the harbor is about eighteen feet, channels are dredged to more than twice that. Soundview Park in the Bronx was created by Robert Moses from ship ballast. Newark Bay is now one-third smaller than it was in 1886. Jamaica Bay's mean depth went from three to sixteen feet; Kennedy Airport rests on almost five thousand acres of Jamaica Bay marsh, the fill coming right out of the bay and leaving an unnaturally deep and stagnant hole. The harbor is so well breached that most traverse it with a distinct lack of awareness—few commuters on the Long Island Railroad or the E and F subway lines are cognizant that as they pass through the tunnels to and from Manhattan, they are riding beneath bluefish and barnacles.

2

For a port to function, ships must pass unimpeded. When the water's natural depths exceed the vessels' maximum drafts, there is no problem. But much of New York Harbor was originally shallow. And ships have been growing larger and deeper drafted by the decade.

118

The original seaside entrance to New York Harbor was narrow, the complex currents and tides having trapped vast loads of sand and silt. Most of the Lower New York Bay was mudflats and shoals. The west bank stretched from Staten Island's southeastern shore deep into the Lower Bay and the east bank, exposed at low tide, was a three-mile-wide rectangle that extended south to within a half mile of Sandy Hook. The *Halfmoon*, which drew eight feet of water, had difficulty entering the bay and on a falling tide had to follow the east bank southward from Breezy Point until she met the stronger current and greater depths of the natural Sandy Hook Channel, which allowed her to pass through the gap between the east and west banks.

Dredging was not possible until later, but in the 1770s ship captains wishing to navigate through the Lower New York Bay benefited from the DesBarres's Atlantic Neptune chart series; this incorporated delicately rendered drawings of the coastline and the entrances to important harbors, including New York's. These images, called recognition views, portrayed landmarks in the correct alignments for safe passage down the channels. One line on the chart showed the direction to align the view, and a second line provided the angle to follow—better than nothing, but only workable under salubrious conditions. Still, when conditions were good during those preindustrial days, they were very good. Danckaerts reported that skippers sailing along the coast in clear weather could make out the Catskill Mountains some 112 miles inland.

In 1830 the maximum weight of vessels was only about one thousand tons, and their greatest draft did not exceed eighteen to twenty feet. By 1855 maximum tonnage was four times greater and ships drew twenty-one to twenty-three feet. But at that same time the natural depth at low water over the bar at Sandy Hook was just twenty-four feet, and something needed to be done about it.

The Flood Rock explosion at Hell Gate, 1885. (From *Bight of the Big Apple*, source: Museum of the City of New York)

Opening the Long Island Sound route to New York Harbor so "provokingly barred" at Hell Gate was a favored option because it would avoid a hundred-mile exposure to a dangerous ocean coast, shorten the route to Europe by fifty miles, and eliminate the wait for high water at Sandy Hook. Soft-bottom dredging at that time was done by specially rigged vessels that scooped sediments; however, the bedrock of Hell Gate offered a challenging exception. One briefly considered alternative to deepening Hell Gate was to dig a ship canal around it through Astoria, a neighborhood in the borough of Queens. But Hell Gate's most dangerous reefs surrendered to enormous blasts in 1876 and 1885; the latter used six times more dynamite than had ever been previously fired in the world, sent geysers 250 feet into the air, and may have been the biggest explosion prior to the atomic bomb. That blast of 1885 shattered the bedrock to the thirty-foot level, creating cracks wide enough for divers to enter and allowing excavation to the desired channel depth of twenty-six feet. Hallett's Reef, which protruded three hundred feet into the river, was weakened before blasting by tunneling and excavating from below. Other reefs in the Hell Gate gauntlet were shaved with multiple small explosions.

In the end the overriding importance of the busiest port in the country provided sufficient impetus to open the other end of the harbor anyway. By 1884 a thirty-foot-deep channel was carved through the Sandy Hook–Breezy Point transect, but by 1897 even this was inadequate for the ten-thousand-ton steamers that were becoming commonplace; thirty-five feet became the new goal. In 1899 Congress authorized funds for a forty-foot channel two thousand feet in width. A new seven-mile path was chosen, along the East Channel across Sandy Hook bar, and it was named the

Excavation at Hell Gate.

Ambrose Channel after John Wolfe Ambrose, the Irish physician who lobbied Congress for eighteen years for funds to create the channel but died before it was dredged. The Ambrose Channel remains the main passage to New York Harbor to this day, but now at forty-five feet.

The New York and New Jersey bistate Port Authority was founded in 1921 with the mission of promoting commerce of the port. Long known for its arrogance toward the environment, it has of late converted to the view that the success of the port is closely tied to the quality of the estuary. The Port Authority now operates seven marine terminals, including three of the biggest in the world, at Port Newark and Port Elizabeth as well as Howland Hook, Staten Island. But maintaining the preeminent position of the Port of New York against the competition of Norfolk, Baltimore, and Halifax for the business of huge container ships has become a serious challenge because of environmental concerns about dredging. In 1996 there were 4,636 ship calls to the Port of New York, with 1.1 million containers handled and a total general and bulk cargo of more than fifty-five million tons—about one-quarter of all U.S. maritime trade. Cargo through the port is expected to quadruple over the next forty years, but only if the giant loaded vessels can pass through the harbor.

In earlier times when economic interests ruled over what little environmental consciousness existed, dredge spoils were simply dumped at sea. It's not so simple anymore—almost all of the sediments of New York Harbor are too contaminated to be legally deposited in the ocean. The central problem is finding a final repository for the three million tons of mud that rains down each year on the channels. Between one and four million tons of sediment annually pass through the Hudson estuary and New York

Harbor. A large fraction of this settles during the spring freshet. The typical amount of sediment suspended in the water in low-flow conditions is about twenty milligrams per liter; during extreme flows following heavy downpours this may increase fifty-fold. Siltation rates can be extraordinary: A sediment trap near Hudson River Pier 76 showed eight inches of accumulation over a ninety-day period, for an astonishing rate of almost one yard per year. But these traps don't release sediments that might naturally be scoured again.

Sophisticated radionuclide studies, however, confirm what common sense suggests. That is, despite the large amounts of sand, mud, and silt being carried down the Hudson River and high sedimentation rates in the harbor, deposition in the harbor is approximately equal with scouring (otherwise the harbor would have filled with sand and mud). Single sedimentation events in the harbor may be large and local rates may be high, but the net change is essentially no change as new deposits become redistributed and move out of the system.

Nonetheless the channels must be dredged to forty-five feet (and soon to forty-seven feet to accommodate cargo ships measuring more than one thousand feet long) and the sediments disposed of. For more than seventy-five years dredged materials were transported to the "Mud Dump" in the New York Bight several miles offshore of Sandy Hook. Ironically, the "hits" on the Mud Dump were more precise when the regulations concerning it were looser. Before it was closed to regular use it was defined as a discrete one-by two-mile box, which was often missed by dump-vessel captains. But prior to that ships only had to go past an imaginary transect some distance from the harbor. With no incentive to go farther, captains would dump as soon as they passed the line. This resulted in a series of little man-made mountains on the bottom as the transect was moved outward into the bight over the years. One of these was called Mount Spike because of the way it looked on depth-recording machines; this mound of sediment from Newark Bay reached to within twenty feet of the surface and was a navigation hazard.

Now all dredge spoils undergo rigorous tests that involve direct measurements of their toxic components, of lethality of mud samples to amphipods, and of twenty-eight-day uptake of contaminants to clams and worms. If the sediments pass these hurdles, they may be jettisoned at HARS—the Historic Area Remediation Site, basically the old Mud Dump—under the theory that this somewhat-clean material will cap the older noxious matter. The operation costs about two dollars per cubic yard. If the sediments fail these tests, alternatives must be found, and all of them tried to date are expensive. One option is to keep them in the harbor in "nearshore containment areas." Such locations are scarce. Borrow pits—another possibility—are the holes left underwater after sediments are removed. To place sediments in a borrow pit in Newark Bay, however, costs thirty dollars per cubic yard. The harbor's port industry is desperate for additional options. Some of the material is being used as fill in strip mines in Pennsylvania. Some treated sediment forms a new sixty-foot-high mountain along the Hackensack River in Kearny. Some is tucked under a parking lot in Elizabeth and in gradings along New Jersey highways. And some dead-end areas in Jamaica Bay and Flushing Bay are being looked at covetously by dredge-spoil managers.

Dredging is also driving further pollution-reduction efforts. With such a cost disparity between offshore and all other forms of disposal, the economic incentive to make sure newly dredged sediments pass muster is great. Hence, CARP—the Contamination and Assessment Reduction Project. CARP is a rather enlightened federal and bistate program designed to turn off the smallest spigots of toxic chemicals to the harbor under the realization that all contamination ultimately finds its way into the sediments.

One long-term trend bodes well for the harbor's dredging problem. The evolution of land use in the Hudson Valley suggests less sediment is pouring into the river. Erosion runoff to the river is greatest from agricultural lands where the earth is literally chewed up. Although a great deal of the Hudson Valley has been suburbanized, agriculture has shrunk substantially, and much of this once-farmed land is reverting to earth-gripping forest. So the trend should be toward a clearer river and less sedimentation—and, hopefully, less frequent dredging.

3

To many, the Hackensack River is a joke—a meandering eyesore, a tidal creek soaked with the effluvium of decades of industrial abuse and runoff from the Secaucus pig farms and landfilled willy-nilly for development, its shores laden with so much illegally dumped refuse that it would combust spontaneously on hot, windy days, the smoldering trash sending environmental smoke signals that were easily interpreted but long ignored. Still, a few did care and now see something more: "This is my Mississippi, my Amazon," says Bill Sheehan as he steers his floating classroom, an "Aquapatio" party barge, down one of the Hackensack River's side channels. Bill is the Hackensack's keeper, in both the official and biblical senses.

A child of the Hackensack Meadowlands, Sheehan grew up as an "Irish gypsy," passing through eight apartments scattered around it. Whether he lived in Secaucus, squarely in the great marsh, or in Union or Jersey City Heights at its edges, Sheehan romped through the Meadowlands as a Boy Scout and on his own. His mother would warn, "Bill, you'll sink into that place someday and they'll never find you!" Sheehan managed to remain on terra semi firma and eventually became a local expert and champion of the Hackensack River system.

Keeperhood came unexpectedly. New York Harbor has its own keeper, Andy Willner, the New York/New Jersey Harbor Baykeeper, the self-proclaimed "mouth of the harbor." Keepers are people who dedicate themselves to protecting a water body. The notion was borrowed and extended by Robert H. Boyle, who observed that British salmon rivers had keepers who kept an eye on the poachers eyeing the runs. Boyle helped establish the Hudson Riverkeeper, a romantic position of broad advocacy that includes patrolling the river to find pollution or other environmental outrages and instigating lawsuits against the guilty parties. So successful was the concept that Boyle could have sold keeperhood franchises; there now are keepers for Long Island Sound, the Delaware River, and San Francisco Bay, and even a Reefkeeper in Florida—almost three dozen nationwide at last count.

Willner realized he could extend his reach by creating a Baykeeper Auxilliary: highly motivated amateur environmentalists from other walks of life who spend time on and care about the harbor. Bill Sheehan, then a taxi dispatcher, became Willner's eyes on the Hackensack River, finally taking over the lead on some Hackensack issues. Although the keepers never did establish a franchise system, they came close when they organized as the National Alliance of River, Sound, and Baykeepers, a body that has licensed the use of the term *keeper*. Keepers have a way of arising organically from the waters and muck that spawn them. Willner brought Sheehan to a national meeting and surprised him by letting him have the floor during a "sharing," in which the keepers report on their activities. Unprepared, he gave a five-minute synopsis that so moved the others that one of them said, "I guess we have a new keeper here." When I met him Sheehan's enthusiasm showed in his garb—nouveau pirate environmentalist—which included mutton chops, an earring, gold chains with anchor and turtle pendants, ecology pins on his hat, and a SAVE OUR WETLANDS message across his T-shirt.

The Meadowlands could easily be the national symbol of environmental resilience. Even today, in its much improved state, because of the routing of sewers that dump into the lower Hackensack, the upper Hackensack River can be more saline than the lower river, nearer the sea. Before industry, pig farms, and land-filling, the Meadowlands stretched for more than twenty thousand acres and included a dense forest of forty- to sixty-foot-tall white cedars that covered an area of the valley larger than Central Park and provided a retreat not only for huge flocks of cedar waxwings but also for various buccaneers, who terrorized harbor traffic. The cedar trees provided a simple solution to traveling across the quaggy terrain. I had driven to Sheehan's dock on Paterson Plank Road. Although asphalted, it was named when it was one of three plank roads through the Meadowlands built by early European settlers. And what an unpleasant, bone-jarring ride it must have been. The cedar timbers were split and laid crosswise to form a solid-wood thoroughfare, but to stop the logs from sinking into the mud (even modern asphalt roads buckle and settle in the Meadowlands), they were placed flat-side down, leaving the semicircular arches for the wood and metal wagon wheels to bump across. Timbering, together with diking and ditching (which changed salinity and flowage patterns), destroyed the cedars; they were gone by 1900. Today the only evidence of these forests are stumps along the riverbanks.

Restoration of even a small cedar forest in the Meadowlands is a recurring dream. Twice it's been attempted on a large scale by the Hackensack Meadowlands Development Commission. On the first bid small saplings were planted, which proved irresistible to the muskrats of the marsh. Taller stock was tried next, and these trees survived until a large storm breached a dike, drowning them with fatal salt water.

We putter up the Hackensack and Sheehan steers his tour boat, reverentially named the *Robert H. Boyle*, eastward up a tributary, Overpeck Creek. Diamondback terrapins, a brackish-water turtle rampantly overharvested for a turn-of-the-century gourmet food fad and scarce until recently, slide off the mud banks to the water. Sheehan points out a side creek that was created years earlier as mitigation by Hartz Mountain Corporation for a development project. Deepening or making new channels has the effect of increasing circulation and allowing ecologically productive spartina grass to grow. In the distance three orange backhoes loom high over the flat landscape, carving out another creek. Hartz Mountain, the primary Meadowlands landowner, once had grand development plans for the marsh, including a two-hundred-acre fill with an office complex and two thousand "synergistic apartment" units for the workers. But a carrot and a stick caused a retreat on their part: Inner-city economic incentives and environmental hurdles have reoriented their corporate attention to urban sites. Sheehan turns the boat around under the New Jersey Turnpike bridge over Overpeck Creek, but not before he points out swallow nests overhead—mud cocoons plastered to girders— inches above which passes much of New Jersey's humanity.

Sheehan already has played a role in assuring the preservation of the remaining Meadowlands. While he hosted Mayor Anthony Just of Secaucus on a cruise, the mayor asked what he could do to help. Sheehan's response was, "Just buy it!"—which he later came to consider "one of the most important flippant remarks I ever made." Not long after, Hartz Mountain Corporation asked for a real estate tax reduction based on a new but lowered assessment of four thousand dollars per acre, due to decreased development prospects. The mayor saw his chance and surprised the company by responding, "I'll buy it!" He then brokered a purchase by the Hackensack Meadowlands Development Commission of 186 acres.

Continuing down the Hackensack we pass a large johnboat overloaded with fish traps. This is the mother ship of an enterprise named Kenny's Killer Killifish, a fearsome-sounding name for a two-inch minnow. Most anglers who drift live killifish for fluke bait in the clear-water inlets along the Jersey shore have no inkling

Snake Hill, New Jersey Meadowlands. (John Waldman)

that they originate from traps parked in the murky but fertile marsh drains of the Meadowlands. We then come upon the area's only natural vertical relief, Snake Hill, an improbable mountain of volcanic rock that is related geologically to the Palisades. Snake Hill was named for its once-robust snake population—the expansive Meadowlands offered happy hunting for snakes, but almost nowhere to den except in the crevices of Snake Hill. Indeed, the snakes were so numerous in the marsh that they were responsible for naming Secaucus, which means "place of snakes" in the Native dialect. Snake Hill also has been despoiled, most of its northern face having been removed for traprock, the blasting not ceasing until the vibrations wobbled the local bridges.

We also pass Harmon Cove, a condominium complex on the river that offers prospective buyers as a main attraction a private marina on a cul-de-sac. But the Meadowlands are saying that maybe development doesn't belong here. Not only is the substrate sinking around the well-anchored buildings, but the marina's slips now sit out of the water on mud, bereft of boats. No provision was made to guard the facility against the Hackensack's heavy sediment load, and the quay is now nothing but a silting backwater— an incipient marsh, the Meadowlands counterpunching. Sheehan floats the *Robert H. Boyle* with the rising tide into the Sawmill Marsh, a tidal channel and wetland that is the Eden of this region of the Meadowlands. Once part of the system of gates and dikes that controlled water movement through the Meadowlands, the Sawmill Marsh breached in the 1951 hurricane and never was repaired because there were no commercial interests behind it. Since then, as in Harmon Cove, it has been reclaiming itself toward a natural state, setting an example that Sheehan interprets as "telling us what the entire Meadowlands wants to be." The

Sawmill Marsh scampers with life—a pocket-sized northern Everglades with reed-lined side channels covered with fiddler crab colonies and terrapins, and large mudflats showing a sampling of the remarkable 260 species of birds found in the Meadowlands.

The future of the thirty-two-square-mile Meadowlands district is largely under the control of the Development Commission, which has three remarkably contradictory missions: to protect nature, to provide for orderly development, and to provide space for the disposal of solid waste. As such, the commission has proposed a "special area management plan" that concedes some development but also limits the acreage that could be filled and secures more than eight hundred million dollars from developers for environmental restoration. Nonetheless environmentalists are not keen on the potentially precedent-setting proposal by the Mills Corporation of Arlington, Virginia, to build yet another shopping mall in New Jersey, the state's largest, right on 206 acres of federally protected Meadowlands marsh, a privilege the company wishes to obtain by agreeing to restore 380 acres in the rest of the wetlands. The typical developers-versus-environmentalists standoff has ensued.

4

No waterfront project focused as much attention on the ecology of the harbor as the proposal to build a new West Side Highway along the Hudson River shore of Manhattan from the Brooklyn Battery Tunnel north to Forty-second Street. The need for replacement was underscored when in December 1973 a portion of the elevated highway collapsed and two vehicles fell to the pavement below. Called Westway for short, the plan for the new road had two features that roiled the blood of environmentalists: It would have

131

filled 242 acres of the Hudson River—an unambiguous ecological affront—and some of the newly created land was slated for luxury apartment buildings—a serious social-policy faux pas. The text of the environmental impact statement for a 1973 study for Westway spoke of the area as "biologically impoverished," but the field study that the impact statement was drawn from completely contradicted that notion. The U.S. National Marine Fisheries Service, the U.S. Fish and Wildlife Service, and the Environmental Protection Agency all voiced concerns about the project and persuaded the New York State Department of Transportation to fund another biological study of the Westway reach.

This penultimate study, begun in 1979, was more substantial and it, too, showed an abundant and diverse fish community. But at its end the Army Corps of Engineers recommended issuance of the crucial landfill permit. This was met with lawsuits by the Sierra Club and allied groups such as the Clean Air Campaign, questioning the adequacy and legality of the environmental review process. Shortly after federal judge Thomas Griesa voided the landfill permit granted by the Army Corps, the tactics of the Westway supporters became more ham-handed. In December 1982 Colonel M. W. Smith Jr. of the Army Corps announced there would be no more fish studies and that he intended to issue the permit. Awkwardly, the Army Corps was forced to rescind Smith's verdict when it became known that he was seeking a job with Parsons, Brinckeroff & Quade—the main engineering consultant for Westway—as he deliberated those decisions. New York's Governor Mario Cuomo then took his support to the U.S. Congress, where amendments to exempt Westway from the fundamental and court-ordered environmental review process were introduced in both the House and the Senate.

After much legal and political wrangling, the conflict culminated in an agreement late in 1983 by the Army Corps of Engineers to sponsor an intensive two-year study of the ecological importance of the Westway reach, a study that would include as its basis of comparison the rest of the harbor, western Long Island Sound, and the Hudson River to Peekskill. And although credence in ecological science demands replication of a study across at least two years in order to account for natural variability among years, political pressure quickly reduced the length of the study to a scant four months of winter.

The New Jersey Marine Sciences Consortium won the Westway contract, and crews of biologists were immediately rounded up. When I got the call, I was a financially struggling doctoral student teaching part time and manning a shift in a restaurant serving chimichangas and enchiladas; most of the others were out-of-work graduates of marine biology programs. There was a palpable sense that we were pawns in an exercise aimed at getting the study over with—we were trained in a matter of days, issued orange survival suits in case we slipped overboard, and scattered among several vessels.

All winter we combed the bottom with trawl nets, enjoying an intimate look at the estuary at a time of year that traditionally has been avoided by scientists. Although hauling nets in a fifteen-degree nor'wester may be good for the soul, it stings the flesh; still, the harbor was ours, and the solitude in these narrow aquatic corridors at the center of a megalopolis was a revelation. During midwinter we set out to trawl a series of stations from Manhattan to Peekskill just as a hard freeze was sweeping the Hudson. As we worked our way upriver, ice floes yielded to solid but thin ice, no challenge for the prow of our steel catamaran, the *Atlantic Twin*.

At night, the vessel secured, I lay exhausted in my bunk with my ear near the hull and fell asleep to the hammer and crunch of tide-driven ice against metal. Heading back to our Jersey City port after the two-day sortie, we encountered much thicker ice. Night fell as the captain picked his way through the ice fields. The boat hands and biologists gathered in the darkened wheelhouse and watched silently as the *Atlantic Twin* would be stymied, only to back up and charge again. As we chewed our way downriver, the rime-covered surface glowed with blue light reflected from the densely popu-lated shores, but in the middle of the lower Hudson we felt as alone as polar explorers.

Part of the study involved towing trawl nets straight down the channel off Manhattan, but we also needed to estimate the abun-dances of fish between and alongside the piers—the very heart of the issue. To do this, we backed the *Twin* right up to Manhattan sidewalks—surprising pedestrians—dropped the net over, and then gunned the engines, hoping to get the trawl to spread its fish-gathering mouth before it passed the pier-head line. I was fortu-nate to have been assigned to the larger vessels. One crew was given the heroic task of pulling a small trawl net in the lanes between piling rows under a large Manhattan pier. Improvising in the icy darkness, they found they could drag the net behind the bow of the tiny aluminum skiff operated in reverse. That is, until a large, fast-moving ship passed down the channel, when they would grimly hang on to the nearest pilings as rollers from the vessel's wake smashed through the field of timbers.

At times we were entertained by the diversions the harbor offered. We saw two floaters during Floaters' Week and none the rest of the study. Towing the net around Manhattan yielded old bottles; entire trees; bows, planks, and other pieces of ships;

Landing a file cabinet in trawl net, Westway Study. (John Waldman)

enough metal furniture to outfit an office building; rotted carp dumped from a market; stuffed garbage bags that we were afraid to open; and a dead dog. I claimed a wooden ship's oak stave we pulled up near the Spuyten Duyvil; swollen after a century or more underwater, it later shrank by half. We caught a sturgeon wearing a rubber band around what would have been its neck, if it had one. This not rare phenomenon occurs when a sturgeon, rooting through the sediments, pokes its snout through a rubber band or torn condom, which, over time, rolls backward along its body. On our specimen the band had become trapped by the fish's pectoral fins, girdling its body as it grew.

Before days spent near Manhattan's West Side piers we looked forward to the characters they attracted. Although the symbolism of his activities escaped us, the "flagman" was special—wrapped in a large American flag, he'd walk to the end of a pier, unfurl the red,

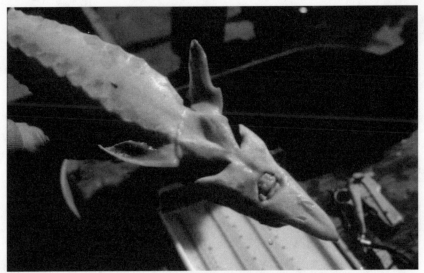

Atlantic sturgeon girdled by a rubber band. (John Waldman)

white, and blue, and then wave his penis at New Jersey. To help break the tension surrounding this grim, carefully watched study, when observers or inspectors were on board I'd discreetly drop a realistic-looking plastic human hand into the net before it was fished; while it was towed, I'd discuss the possibilities of catching cadavers. Perhaps it was just our cold-benumbed minds, but we found it fiendishly delightful to see the guests leap halfway across the deck when they spotted fingers among the fish.

About fifty-five species of fish were caught in the Westway sampling effort, but all eyes were on the star of the show—striped bass. As with many ecological studies, our results were highly equivocal. Young stripers certainly were abundant along the Westway piers, but they also were numerous elsewhere in the lower Hudson, as far north as Yonkers. Perhaps the most important reason the Westway construction permit was ultimately denied was that there was no

agreed-upon decision-making criterion to be applied to the results
of the survey. Rather, a single Army Corps of Engineers biologist
was given the task of rapidly interpreting the mountainous data. His
preliminary findings were released in a draft supplemental environmental impact statement in which he concluded that landfilling of
the Westway reach would have a significant impact on the Hudson
River striped bass population, projecting a possible loss of 20 to 33
percent of juveniles. Although the final environmental impact statement lacked the word *significant*, the Army Corps was unable to
backtrack from its initial position. Despite this, and despite enormous, mostly negative public comment and strong objections from
the other federal agencies, the new Army Corps colonel in charge,
Bud Griffis, announced his intent to approve the Westway landfill
permit. In August 1985 lawsuits threw the issue back to Judge
Griesa. Griesa once again voided the landfill permit while barely
containing his disdain for the arrogance for due process displayed by
Westway advocates and for the Army Corps' actions and findings,
using terms such as *incredible, bizarre,* and *sheer fiction* in his written
opinion. Mercifully, the project was abandoned by Governor
Cuomo and Mayor Koch in September 1985.

Although the West Side Highway Project is dead, Westway-
type issues along New York City's waterfront have not gone away.
Landfilling of the river bottom became out of the question, but
some prodigious piling-supported structures were built: the
Waterside complex in the East River rests in part on six acres of
pilings; the largest pile-supported structure in the estuary is the
North River Sewage Treatment Facility on an astonishing thirty
acres of concrete cylinders between 137th and 145th Streets along
the Hudson River. But what are the biological effects of these
forests of pilings in what previously had been open water?

The environmental thrust of water pollution couldn't be more apparent: Increased contamination is bad, lessened contamination is good. But the present ecological value of the artificial habitats that make up the shell of New York Harbor, which comprise a complete reengineering so far from the pristine starting point that it seems they could only represent a drastic decline in condition and yet host myriad life, is the great scientific mystery of the harbor. Not only is it difficult to determine the extent of biological change as a consequence of habitat alterations, but it's also a challenge simply to determine the direction of change. Does placement of a small pier on the flat, silty bottom off the West Side of Manhattan augment or diminish that habitat? Is it reasonable to assume that the pier would add desirable complexity to a relatively featureless locale? If so, would a giant platform be of greater benefit or would negative effects also be seen? No one knows the answers to these fundamental questions. The Wall Street crash of 1987 and subsequent slack economy eased what had been intense development pressure on the waterfront, leaving a Mexican standoff in its wake. Developers want to be told what they have to do to assuage environmentalists and satisfy regulators, cynically considering it part of the cost of doing business. Arch-environmentalists defend against any change to the status quo, as if through providence the harbor's present infrastructure is optimal for its creatures. Regulators remain as confused as they were during the Westway battles, largely because so little research is performed on these questions.

Reliable quantitative sampling of sea life—that is, detecting a trustworthy ecological signal—has been the dilemma in determining the value of these pile-supported structures as habitat. It is nearly impossible to pull a net through the narrow, refuse-filled, cross-membered corridors between the piles; worse yet, anywhere nets can be pulled under piers may be considered atypical of them.

Through serendipitous circumstances, another way was found to delve this issue. I had been appointed to the Habitat Committee of the New York/New Jersey Harbor Estuary Program. The main item on the agenda for an upcoming meeting was to develop the Advanced Identification Process, nicknamed AVID, an idea being avidly advanced by the Environmental Protection Agency to learn more about the biological and physical worlds of piers before permit applications to build or modify them were submitted. Although this proactive approach was better than doing nothing at all, it wasn't real science—there was no hypothesis testing involved. It was more of a "let's measure as much as we can and then form some opinions" approach—highly subjective at best.

On the way to the AVID meeting I happened to be reading proposals to the Hudson River Foundation. Among them was one from Dr. Kenneth Able of Rutgers University, who wished to compare fish habitats in lower New York Harbor and New Jersey using a simple but innovative approach: the growth of caged fish and the numbers of young fish caught in traps as indicators of habitat value. It struck me that this was an excellent way to get around the problems of pulling nets in and around piers. It also lent itself to hypothesis testing—one could test for all-important statistical differences between the underpier environment and control sites, such as nearby waters of the same depth halfway between piers. Although many subscribe to the view that there are "lies, damned lies, and then statistics," reliance on statistical tests is the absolutely necessary baseline of good science (and courtroom science).

At the meeting I introduced the notion of trying to convince Able to adapt his approach to this pressing urban issue. The group immediately sensed the advantages. Although Able, a highly focused researcher, was a bit reticent to plunge into such politically shark-infested waters, he agreed to try it. Marcy Benstock, one of the primary Westway dragon slayers (together with Albert Butzel), fiercely opposed the study, perhaps because she sensed that an absence of scientific information gave her anti-Manhattan shoreline development coalition a better hand to play, and she mounted a campaign to derail it.

But the project eventually did proceed, and it quickly began to yield absolutely new insights. One day I climbed into a workboat to see the underpier environment firsthand with Able's primary assistant on the study, postdoctoral associate Dr. Janet Duffy-Anderson, and a student guy Friday, Charles Metzger. We loaded the bow with specially designed fish cages and motored to Hudson River Pier 40, a massive platform eight hundred feet long and one thousand feet wide that once berthed ocean liners of the Holland-America line and was recently considered as a site for a new Guggenheim Museum.

Some of the locations where the cages were to be dropped were far under the pier. Metzger steered the boat down one of the alleys between the pilings and it rapidly darkened, with only the soft cavelike glow of a distant light source. The steel girders were rusty and covered with a patina of algae and salt. Here and there were openings to the top of the pier, and we glimpsed the hubcaps of the cars and buses parked there. Over our heads hung stalactites—gray icicles of unknown substances, perhaps a slow distillation of the chemical essence of New York City. All that was missing were bats—such a habitat might be attractive to them, if salt water produced the insect hatches bats thrive on. But barn swallows nest under the piers, and night-herons sometimes pass their days there.

Measuring underwater light transmission under Hudson River Pier 40. (John Waldman)

Below Pier 40 or any other large Manhattan pier would be a great place to hide if on the lam—the isolation and otherworldliness are disrupted only by the rare engineering inspection or weekend kayakers who use the pilings as slalom courses.

We removed our test animals—young-of-the-year winter flounder held in a water-filled cooler, the fish nearly white in their attempt to match their background. They were to be placed, three to a cage, at sites under the pier and between piers, and then retrieved hours later to see what and how much they had eaten of the local prey—a final component to a study that was by this time focusing on whether differences in apparent habitat value between underpier and interpier areas were due to differences in food or in light availability. Duffy-Anderson dropped a sensitive illumination meter to the bottom under Pier 40. Despite the mere nine-foot depth and

141

bright noontime sunshine, light is barely detectable there—it often is two orders of magnitude less than outside the pier.

In the end four years of study by Able and his colleagues in the lower Hudson River showed clear differences in growth and the numbers of fish trapped among underpier, interpier, and open pile fields lacking platforms, but surprisingly the responses were highly species-specific: A fish is not a fish is not a fish. Striped bass, winter flounder, and tautog grow best and are most numerous in open pile fields, and all three grow slowest and are scarcest under piers. However, tomcod show little variation among the three habitat types, and eels are most abundant under piers. These differences indicate that light may be a crucial factor, with those fish adept at feeding in low-light conditions managing to endure in the piers' eternal darkness. Thus, the ecological signal from the biota has become a little clearer but also more complex; for now developers, environmentalists, and regulators will remain locked in their less-than-holy trinity.

The paralysis that, since the Westway battle, has gripped the once-doomed stretch of the Hudson from Fifty-ninth Street to the Battery has begun to yield to a middle ground under the aegis of the Hudson River Park Alliance, led by Albert Butzel and made up of about thirty-five institutions including the Environmental Defense Fund, Natural Resources Defense Council, Municipal Art Society, Parks Council, and Trust for Public Land. Although Butzel was pleased to help slay the Westway monster, he did not imagine that as part of his legacy an enormous length of Manhattan's Hudson River shoreline would remain gripped by controversy and largely unusable by the public for fifteen years. His compromise, a mixed-use park, results from a delicate and shifting détente among many environmental and municipal groups, and it satisfies neither developers nor ardent foes such as the Clean Air Campaign or the Sierra Club. Much of its appeal is based on the notion that something is far better than nothing. The conflict between the environmental extremists and moderates over the final state of the park has been aptly described as pitting the "perfect against the good."

5

Habitat is the new environmental mantra of the coastal zone now that the battle for better water quality is winding down. To pay attention to habitat concerns might appear straightforward—but the problem is that "habitat science," particularly of the urban variety, is not well developed, and what constitutes beneficial habitat is largely in the eye of the beholder. Moreover, what is good for one set of animals may not be good for another. Nonetheless habitat that is blatantly bad, Newtown Creek for instance, is unequivocal. So is good habitat apparent, such as Shooters Island, at least for a wide spectrum of birds.

But in this well-peopled estuary much of the harbor bottom and uplands suffer from modifications, mixed uses, and, as such, present habitats of only marginal quality. With the awakening of habitat consciousness, fresh sources of money have poured into government agencies, allowing new opportunities for proactive habitat restoration, opportunities that may at times exceed the clear need for such work. It is not always obvious when a habitat is good enough as is, whether it should be left alone to heal naturally, what could be done to improve it, or whether a makeover is truly an improvement. Most habitat restoration efforts have focused on re-creating tidal wetlands—a kind of habitat that was once opportunistically thought of as wasteland ripe for "reclamation" as filled land but is now viewed as the shining wheat fields of coastal food chains. It's not hard to make a case for restoring this particular environment: About sixty-one thousand acres of tidal marshes have been lost in New York Harbor, and twenty-one thousand out of a possible twenty-five thousand acres in New York alone. Manhattan had its share of these wetlands, more than six hundred acres. The Ratzer Map, published in 1776, shows an enormous salt meadow north of Corlears Hook on the East River that reached north to about Thirteenth Street far into Manhattan—a single farm occupied a high spot deep in the marsh near the intersection today of Ninth Street and Avenue C. (The mosquitoes of these salt marshes were horrific; at night some Manhattan residents' faces became so badly swollen from mosquito bites that, the next day, they were ashamed to go out in public.)

At Inwood—the very northern end of Manhattan, facing the big *C* painted on a rock cliff over the Harlem River to cheer on the

Derelict vessels in Sherman Creek, Manhattan. (John Waldman)

144

Columbia University sculling team—remains one of Manhattan's relict salt marshes, an example of what Elizabeth Barlow in *The Forests and Wetlands of New York City* termed a parcel of patri- archical ecology. Once billed by the Inwood Heights Park Alliance as Manhattan's last salt marsh, it is not now a terribly convincing example of one, consisting mainly of a thin ring of phragmites bor- dering a broad mudflat and a run of spartina down a shallow canal, but by end-of-the-century Gotham standards it verges on the spectacular. However, if one is to grant salt marsh status to this tame little cove, then there is a second, less celebrated salt marsh in Manhattan, at the mouth of Sherman Creek. Tucked into the borough's northeast corner, this reed-lined cul-de-sac sits behind a marina near the head of the Harlem River Expressway. Once a broad waterway that stretched across much of Manhattan Island, Sherman Creek is now but an open sore in the bank of the Harlem River, filled by a fleet of rotting vessels and a generous allotment of flotsam, with a greasy service station spanning the gap where its tides once ebbed and rose.

Spartina is to a salt marsh what coral is to a coral reef. Living coral resides on the skeletons of dead coral, the combination of the two creating a home for a unique set of animals. Similarly, spar- tina grows on the peat formed by the accretion of grass over time, and this habitat hosts its own biota. At higher elevations in areas less flooded by seawater, *Spartina patens* grows. This short, matted grass is known as salt hay and was used by Dutch colonists in Brooklyn and Queens as cattle fodder. Because of the high value of buildable shoreline real estate, little *S. patens* occurs around New York Harbor anymore. Seaward of salt hay grows salt marsh cord- grass, *S. alterniflora*, a much coarser and taller species that spends considerably more time submerged. That spartina, descended from terrestrial plants, can tolerate salt water is testimony to its unique adaptations—the two species are the only land plants that thrive in the east coast's salty waters. The problem for land vegetation in contact with salt water is osmosis—the tendency for water to flow across cell membranes from the less salty interior of the plant to the outside, leaving the plant drained and flaccid. Spartina has evolved an elegant solution: It concentrates salts until its cells are more saline than salt water. And it does this innocuously. The particular salts gathered are those that are not otherwise functionally important to the plant. Hence, salt marshes.

Just south of the Goethals Bridge on Staten Island, in the midst of industrial dreck, is a six-acre spartina marsh that hosts the usual complement of killifish, fiddler crabs, mussels, damselflies, ducks, and geese. But Old Place Creek Marsh is an ironic name considering it is now a new place. Marc Matsil proudly led me on a tour. Although it looks natural to the untrained eye, every grass blade in Old Place Creek Marsh stems from plantings coordinated by the Natural Resources Group. The big Exxon oil spill occurred directly across the Arthur Kill from the marsh. Staff and volunteers waded into the oily muck to set young spartina stock started in a nursery on Staten Island. The money to rebuild this marsh came from elsewhere, damage assessments paid by Exxon for its oil spills of 1990. And oily it was. Matsil explained that conventional wisdom had it that marshes with more than five or six thousand parts per million of oil could not be restored. Though portions of this marsh approached ten times that, with the aid of potent doses of time-release fertilizer the plantings took hold, grew three feet in one summer, and even went to seed.

Salt marsh restorations are costly endeavors. At the high end the Hackensack Meadowlands Development Commission estimates

Marsh restoration project, Saw Mill Creek Preserve, Staten Island. (John Waldman)

them at eighty thousand or more dollars per acre. Damage assessment negotiations relying on the nebulous art of contingency evaluation require both sides to place dollar values on wildlife killed. The Arthur Kill with its Fresh Kills landfill does not lack for gulls, and they were assessed at little more than a dime a dozen—actually four for a dollar. But the piping plover, a wisp of a shorebird that is on the federal endangered species list, went for about the cost of a Mercedes, or sixty thousand dollars apiece. Damage assessments from oil spills and other atypical funding sources are supporting marsh restoration at other sites around New York Harbor. But the New York City Department of Parks Natural Resources Group doesn't only depend on local oil spills by Exxon for grant money—it reached as far away as Alaska to win $150,000 in a national grants competition for Exxon Valdez Damages Funds.

147

A much larger restoration is planned for a partially built but then abandoned park just inland of the Hackensack River; it was originally carved out of a wetland. The forthcoming work will essentially reconnect the ninety-acre plot back to the Hackensack, letting the river reclaim it. Other salt marsh restorations are minuscule, such as one planned for the edge of Stuyvesant Town at Twentieth Street on the East River. The slight ecological value of such "pocket marshes," created at unlikely locations, is dramatically outweighed by their educational and symbolic virtues. And a salt marsh expansion is being mapped out in the Spuyten Duyvil to help absorb the spillover from a CSO. The Harbor Estuary Program has picked out more than eighty other sites for restoration efforts that will be ready to go as new funding sources arise.

What of another common kind of New York Harbor habitat, a totally artificial one—the rock-faced wall, often used in the past to retain landfill for development? Before the Westway project was quashed thought was given to lining its waterside with rock, but Westway opponents contended that the wall would be so scoured by currents that life would be excluded from it. To test this theory, in October 1980 two divers, Dr. C. Braxton Dew and Lance Stewart, surveyed the forty-five-foot-tall, sloping rock wall of Battery Park City in waters with a pretty-good-by-harbor-standards seven-foot visibility. Everywhere they looked they saw life. Natural light penetrated to about twenty feet, and snapper bluefish and stripers were seen chasing baitfish among rock crevices, which also housed other fish such as tautog and cunner picking food off the sides like parrotfish on a coral reef. Below that level their flashlight beams revealed winter flounder resting on sediments that ranged from cottony mud more than a yard thick to sand-and-shell bottom. The wall itself was covered with encrusting organisms: barnacles, tunicates or "sea grapes," ghost anemones, sand-builder worms, whelks, and a few oysters. Walking or swimming along the wall were amphipods, sand shrimp, hermit crabs, rock crabs, lady crabs, blue claw crabs, pipefish, and eels. Although this study ultimately didn't win the day for Westway proponents, it did show that the harbor's creatures had little trouble making a living along this man-made structure.

Some habitats, if left alone, erupt in new and original forms. In 1895 Irving T. Bush began development of what became the first "industrial park" in the world. His concept: to integrate the "commercial and industrial functions of manufacturing and warehousing, with both rail and water transportation in one terminal under unified management." During its time it was considered to be one of the economic jewels of New York Harbor. To tour it today is to see rotting piers, chain-link fences, and the bent frames of burned-out buildings. But in 1989 a group of civic volunteers belonging to Sunset Park Restoration secured a grant to study their waterfront and made a startling discovery: Nature had reclaimed it. Forests grew on the piers, and wildlife was evident. The little Sunset Park wilderness, consisting of only two acres of land, fourteen acres of water, and three acres of intertidal pools, is a unique environment along the lengthy stretch of shoreline from the Brooklyn to the Verrazano Bridge. A survey conducted there in 1992 found twenty-three species of birds, including waders, seabirds, birds of prey, and waterfowl; fifteen kinds of fish and shellfish; forty-four types of trees and other vegetation; and even seven different mammals.

The primordial habitat missing from New York Harbor that could really improve its ecology is the oyster reef. Oyster reefs are not merely homes for oysters; the fundamental ecological benefits of oyster beds cannot be overstated. One estimate has it that on a

Staten Island oyster sloop. (Staten Island Historical Society)

per-area basis, oyster reefs remove twenty-five times more nitrogen than do salt marshes. Although no such calculation exists for New York Harbor, the oyster population of the Chesapeake Bay one hundred years ago (prior to its great decline) would have filtered the entire volume of the bay every four to five days. Several oysters placed in a tank of green alga-packed water can clear it in a few hours. The lower Hudson River and New York Harbor are plagued by deposition of fine silt and algae blooms, driven by the excess nutrients humankind generates. These reduce sunlight penetration, making it difficult for eelgrass and seaweed to grow—plants that form important habitats for many young animals. The region's historically vast oyster beds helped clarify the waters, keeping these inputs in a more beneficial ecological balance. Moreover, oyster beds also have myriad crevices and form a shelled jungle that has been found to be consummate habitat for a whole complex of worms, shrimp and other crustaceans, and juvenile and adult fish.

Unfortunately, the ecological role of oysters in New York Harbor has been largely forgotten; given their original distribution and abundance, however, it may be that they were equally as important to the biological workings of the harbor as they were in the Chesapeake Bay. The difference is that in the Chesapeake, the ever-dwindling oyster beds have been fished commercially to the present, and so there is a vocal constituency for conservation projects. But oysters haven't been harvested in New York Harbor for almost a century, and there is little memory of the extensive beds that once dominated its bottom. In the Chesapeake many shore residents garden oysters in floating pens to help cleanse the waters; around New York Harbor some officials discourage the idea of oyster bed restoration because it might create an "attractive nuisance," a short-sighted point of view that suggests the harbor is better off without its native fauna simply to avoid the health risks that might result from any illegal harvest.

The oyster of the harbor and the entire east coast is but one species, *Crassostrea virginica*—the eastern oyster; however, it manifests itself in many local forms with different characteristic shell

151

shapes and meats that vary subtly in flavor. In fact over the course of a year that culinary shrine to oysters, the Oyster Bar at Grand Central Station, offers between fifty-five and seventy kinds of oysters, including "Canadian Coves" from Prince Edward Island, "Bristols" from Maine, "Cotuits" and "Cuttyhunks" from Massachusetts, "Paramour Islands" from Virginia, and "Apalachicolas" from Florida. Another Manhattan restaurant, the Ocean Grille, has an oyster menu that reads like a wine list; various oysters are described as "sweet . . . with a coppery-mineral finish," "briny . . . with a fruity finish," and "robust . . . sweet . . . with a strong cucumber finish." Some of the variability in flavor is due to saltiness; oysters from Long Island Sound may grow up in waters two to three times as saline as those from the Chesapeake Bay. The closest sources of edible oysters to New York Harbor are Cape May, New Jersey; Peconic and Great South Bays; and, yes, Oyster Bay, on Long Island—a radius that sadly disregards an enormous area of former, nearby oyster habitat.

If the waters are not too foul, oysters are remarkably adaptable to local conditions, and their shells offer interpretable clues as to the habitats they came from. In fact the shape of buried oyster shells can reveal the history of a local fishery. At St. Mary's City, Maryland, on the Chesapeake Bay, a researcher retrospectively tracked oyster overharvesting as the community grew in size. The garbage dumps of houses that had exact dates of construction or demolition were excavated in order to estimate the ages of the garbage layers. The earliest oysters were the broadly fan-shaped "cove" oysters that grow solitarily on rocks and rubble on sandy bottoms and that can be picked up at low tide or by wading. As time passed the cove oysters consumed grew smaller and smaller, indicating that they were picked before they could fill out; then abruptly the shape of the shells switched to long, skinny "channel" oysters that had grown deeper and more crowded in the estuary and are harder to obtain.

The New York Harbor oyster industry declined quickly in the late 1800s as contamination and disease compromised the edibility of the remaining oysters. An 1885 survey of the beds near Liberty Island and Fort Washington found a good deal of refuse, as well as oysters with slimy shells and meats that were thin, green, and smelled bad. Nonetheless these reefs might have survived and functioned ecologically even if they weren't harvested. But it appears that they were eclipsed by a torrential rain of sludge. The Metropolitan Sewerage Commission Report for 1910 contains three maps that happen to provide a snapshot of the interplay between the oyster reefs and human wastes. One map shows the pipelines that carried raw sewage to the harbor. Another figure shows the distribution of major sludge deposits that, not surprisingly, correspond well with concentrations of sewer discharges. The third map shows the remaining oyster reefs. Superimpose it on the second map and the remaining oyster reefs appear where sludge doesn't.

In 1976, when a marine archaeologist went diving to look for wrecks of historic importance and, instead, found a small oyster bed around some rotted pilings in the Black Tom Channel area off Liberty State Park in Jersey City, it was considered newsworthy enough to make the front page of one of New York's daily tabloids. Although oysters are seen here and there around the harbor, they are perhaps but a tease of what was and what could be, and they have yet to reestablish any of the large beds that constitute oyster reef habitat. Are conditions subpar for oyster reproduction, or do oysters spawn adequately but then become limited by a lack of hard bottom to attach to or by too much sedimentation?

Ben Longstreth, the New York City arm of the Baykeeper, became fascinated by the possibilities of oyster restoration in New York Harbor. Longstreth looks like his name, a long stretch of a young man, and completely earnest in his many projects to help the harbor, but none so passionately as to bring back oyster reefs. Some ambitious journeys begin with little steps. Oysters in the Hudson estuary begin spawning in late June, and two weeks later the free-floating larvae start searching for a hard place to settle. So in the early summer of 1998 Longstreth set out coarse-mesh bags filled with old oyster shells to trap young oysters, or "spat," at locations all over the harbor to see where they are currently reproducing.

6

It's early October and Longstreth is set to pull up a sack of oyster shells left below the River Project's pier since July. If oysters are naturally breeding in the lower Hudson, there is a good chance that spat have settled as larvae on Longstreth's miniature reef. As the rope is retrieved, more and more colonizing organisms show on it, mostly grayish, squishy sea squirts. The sack comes up all muddy and we rinse it, pouring the runoff through a fine-mesh net. Young oysters are not immediately evident, but it's clear that the pile of shells has served as an attractive habitat for other creatures. We find many grass shrimp, a few young-of-the-year sea bass and cunner, and an abundance of mud crabs. Spreading the shells over the dock, we see more of the same, plus an oyster toadfish, a species so closely associated with oysters that it's named after them. Fleshy and cryptic, toadfish occupy depressions or burrows and dart after and seize prey with their broad jaws. They also are noisy. Houseboaters in Sausalito could not figure out what the strange sounds were that passed through their vessels' hulls at

154

night until a biologist identified them as the love calls of breeding toadfish.

Our expectations that young oysters would be seen are tempered by the generally poor results Longstreth has recorded elsewhere around the harbor with his project—none worse than in the Gowanus Canal. When he hung a sack of live oysters off a bulkhead there, not only were they dead upon his return two weeks later, but the shells had shrunk as well, perhaps because of acidity in the contaminated canal. Careful inspection of the large dead oyster shells now reveals many embryonic forms—apparent oyster spat—and we are excited until on closer examination all turn out to be slipper limpets. Oyster spat, once in place, are attached for life. But the shell of the limpet, a snail-like but highly flattened creature, slips sideways when pushed.

After a great deal of searching and poking, I give up and begin walking back to my office, but when I am almost out of earshot Longstreth yells, "I've got one!" In fact we find three. Not much of an oyster reef, but we are pleased nonetheless.

An artificial oyster reef, built on an appropriately grand scale, just might work in New York Harbor.

5

HOW IS THE HARBOR DOING?

"May the power of the people,
Be heard on each shore;
And bring old Father Hudson,
Clear water once more."

"Old Father Hudson"
Pete Seeger

1

TODAY THE ENVIRONMENT of New York Harbor stands wobbling, but it is growing stronger and steadier, like the survivor of a ghastly medical accident—a healthy victim given chemotherapy and reconstructive surgery for problems she never had. Although the harbor's native biological glory will never be relived, the prognosis is good for recuperation to a satisfactory functional level. And as a result—or maybe as a cause—the body language of the harbor's infrastructure has shifted around: Instead of facing inward, backs to the water, relegating the shore to industry, highways, or just plain decay, cities and towns are now looking toward the harbor, rebuilding the waterfront as an attraction and a refuge, a place to lift the spirit.

Public policy has embraced this momentum. In 1998 the Hudson was designated one of fourteen American Heritage rivers. The New York/New Jersey Harbor Estuary Program has completed its comprehensive plan for managing or at least influencing the environment of the harbor, and some federal dollars for making its recommendations happen are following it. Corporations caught polluting, including Exxon and Consolidated Edison, have paid millions of dollars in settlements called damage assessments that have been transformed into funds to restore habitats, provide access, and educate people about the harbor. Private dollars are also following. The H_2O Fund (for Highlands-to-Ocean) is a consortium of foundations led by the Rockefeller Brothers Fund; it is trying to suture the harbor's environmental, public access, and economic activities into a more seamless whole and, in particular, to reconnect the public with the water.

The public has already begun to rediscover the harbor. Operation Sail, the bicentennial celebration of the United States in 1976, brought millions of people to it to view the parade of tall ships; this event still echoes with the annual Harbor Festival. Esplanades are planned for the old ferry terminal area of Staten Island, the Harlem River in Manhattan, between Riverside Park and Fort Washington Park on the Hudson River, and the Passaic River in downtown Newark; new parks will be created in Stuyvesant Cove in the East River, under the Brooklyn Bridge in Brooklyn, and in Red Hook; a new ferry terminal will be built at Battery Park. The public also shows it cares for the harbor by tidying it; during the 1998 International Coastal Cleanup more than two thousand volunteers cleaned up ninety-two thousand pounds of trash along forty-six of its miles.

Moreover, the harbor has made new friends: Friends of Gateway, Friends of Gerritsen Creek, Friends of the Rockaways,

Friends of Harlem on the River, and other grassroots organizations. Many are reaching for the hearts and minds of children. Floating the Apple runs a summer youth program that takes participants on the water in hand-powered boats and teaches them about the ecology of the lower Hudson. New Settlement Apartments has a Rocking the Boat Program in which students build "Whitehalls"—traditional nineteenth-century harbor skiffs—and then row them on the Harlem River, learning about the waters in the process. At the New York City Outward Bound Center children sail and canoe the Hudson and are educated about the river's ecology, pollution, water quality, and lore. Students even learn about the harbor on the harbor in an old fireboat house on the East River at Eighty-second Street. The sloop *Clearwater* takes school groups out on the Upper New York Bay, the experience heightened by the quiet intimacy with the water achieved by gliding under wind power. Although the young guests enjoy many aspects of these sails, the high point is when the ship's trawl net is brought back on board and they get to watch and handle its catch of the harbor's denizens in the shipboard aquaria.

2

Some teach about the harbor directly by placing a fishing rod in students' hands. Bill Fink, the marine education coordinator for the Battery Park City Parks Conservancy, hosts groups of school-children who cast their lines from the very hub of the harbor—the Battery. In the spring and fall of 1998 alone almost eight hundred participants caught and released 977 fish of nineteen species.

I wanted to see firsthand how students respond to this angling angle. Late November is a harsh time of year to bring novices out on the harbor. But Tom Lake and I are on board to introduce New York City high school students to their own waters in a Friends of

Fishes education program by having them catch and tag striped bass on a large headboat, the *Pastime Princess*. Early on there is little mixing among the two classes—the half that are from Chinatown settle into the bow of the boat and the half from Harlem take the stern. Most of them are completely inexperienced but game; one says in honest amazement, "It's alive!" when he sees the worm bait. Over the course of the day the chill wind thins their ranks; some doze seasick in the cabin, others bop around listening to Walkmen, and some beg, "When are we going back in?" But a portion of each group becomes smitten with the experience and they assemble as one along the stern end of starboard. Coaching and teasing each other, high-fivin' a catch, they excitedly bring their fish to Lake to be tagged, New York Harbor no longer an abstraction in their minds. On the ride back to dock, the only thing missing is Pete Seeger as the students sing the Hudson River ditty "Sailing Up, Sailing Down," much of which seems apropos:

> *Garbage here, garbage there . . .*
> *People come, people go . . .*
> *Some are young, some are old . . .*
> *Catching fish, catching hell . . .*
> *Sailing up, sailing down . . .*
>
> *What did he say?*
> *(The river may be dirty now,*
> *but she's getting cleaner every day.)*

3

How clean she gets remains to be seen. The working of any system has a limiting factor. It's quite clear that human enjoyment of the Hudson River and New York Harbor, the natural right to catch,

eat, and enjoy fish and shellfish without worry that one is poison-
ing oneself, is most limited by the presence of PCBs. Despite
General Electric's public relations spinners, a shameless team that
would make the Clinton White House envious, the pervasiveness
of this contaminant is a black shroud on an otherwise largely
recovered estuary. And although there are local sources of PCBs to
New York Harbor, in the foreseeable future the most important
governmental management decision concerning the system will be
whether to force General Electric to dredge the PCB "hot spots"
upriver and perhaps hasten the estuary's cleansing.

However, in a water body with as long and varied a history of
abuse as New York Harbor, *cleanliness* is a relative term. Centuries
of pollution and habitat destruction drove it to its nadir, and
decades of remediation have partially restored it. But the perspec-
tives of its decision makers are rooted, for the most part, in short
spans of time—the durations of their careers in most instances.
Thus only small portions of the spectrum of change have been
experienced; the horizons viewed don't encompass the entire landscape. As circumstances in the harbor improve today, then, they
compare well with the recent past and we celebrate, but contrast
those conditions to preindustrial times and we have less reason to
be smug.

This syndrome of "shifting baselines" needs to be considered as
we set our environmental goals and standards. And it is rendered
ever more complicated by the natural variation in the ecology of
the harbor that occurs despite our efforts at control. The year 1749
is one that many might assume preceded any noticeable declines in
the sea life of New York Harbor. But that year Peter Kalm spoke
with several fishermen and merchants fifty to sixty years of age
who reported that during their life "they had plainly found several
kinds of fish decrease in number every year; and that they could

not get near so many fish as they could formerly." Was this the normal flux in the availability of certain fish, or was it one of the earliest signals of a soon-to-be-very-stressed harbor?

4

I am often asked, "How is the harbor doing?"—as if the state of such a difficult-to-decipher multifaceted entity can be summed up in a word or two. The state of the harbor is a bit like the stock market: We know it is too big and complex to track in its entirety, and that it is neither as good nor as bad as it can be but fluctuates well within these extremes, and so we look for simple indicators—an environmental Dow Jones index—that provides some useful, if imperfect measure of trends.

Trends from all of the most recent New York City Harbor Survey's indicators are excellent. Fecal coliform bacteria concentrations have declined an order of magnitude since the 1960s because of improved sewage treatment. Shellfishing restrictions were eased on thirty thousand acres of bottom off the Rockaways and in Raritan Bay. Seagate Beach on Coney Island, and South and Midland Beaches on Staten Island, were opened for the first time in decades; as of 1992 all New York City beaches are being swum at again. Members of a new club, the Hudson River Swimmers, do laps between Piers 26 and 32 (although someone once called the harbor police under the assumption that anyone in the water there must have fallen out of a boat). And recent dissolved-oxygen readings have been the highest in eighty years.

Results of the toxics survey of New York Harbor's finfish and shellfish began to arrive in fall 1995. The early returns were encouraging, but with caveats. Of the eighteen kinds of polyaromatic hydrocarbons tested for, none were detected among the winter flounder samples, and only four were found among the soft-shell clams. Levels of dioxins and furans in striped bass and blue claw crabs appeared to drop to less than half of what they'd been ten years earlier. Species that showed high levels of contaminants were usually localized: Anyone eating blue claw crabs from Newark Bay would probably also receive a large dose of dioxin, for instance, while crabs from Jamaica Bay were relatively free of poisons.

In March 1999 the refurbished Gowanus Canal flushing system finally was turned on. The flow, at three hundred million gallons per day, is about equal to a good-sized Catskill Mountain trout stream, minus the fly rodders. Not only can fish be seen in the canal, but the canal's bottom is visible, too. And in June 1999, ten thousand bushels of fossilized oyster shells from Chesapeake Bay were sunk in the very heart of the shellfish's original distribution in New York Harbor, just south of Liberty Island. Orchestrated by Ben Longstreth, it is the harbor's first artificial oyster reef.

Then there are the simplest indicators—the occurrences and abundances of the organisms themselves. Some animals appear to be gone, others don't belong but are here to stay. How do we weigh these changes? What does it mean to the system as a whole that at the beginning of the century we eradicated billions of oysters in the lower estuary, and at the end of the century added billions of zebra mussels in the upper estuary? And sometimes unexpected but originally native species reappear along these urban shores. Should the sight of a sea turtle or capture of an unusual fish be cause for wonder? Perhaps not in these relatively untamed waters if the even more beleaguered animals of the terrestrial world yield similar surprises. (Although a coyote recently turned up in Central Park, it would be easy to argue that the wildest, most inaccessible location within New York City limits is the bottom of Hell Gate.)

John Kieran, in his 1959 work *A Natural History of New York City*, observed that "the curious thing is that the destruction or elimination of plant and animal life in the area through the blanketing of the ground by buildings and pavements is largely a matter of quantity and not of kind." But Kieran may have missed the point concerning abundance. If animals become so scarce that the thread of continuity of their presence becomes broken, then their occasional reappearances become more noteworthy, more symbolic, and more subject to interpretation. We track them in our quest to know "how the harbor is doing," hoping that the frequencies of sightings go up, suggesting a positive trend or, at the very least, a modicum of hope.

In the broadest sense life is the user of water and habitat, and thus life is the great indicator of water quality and habitat suitability and "how the harbor is doing." And the news concerning life in the harbor is cause for optimism—I remain bullish. Sea turtles have been spotted in the Verrazano Narrows and the East River. A pair of bottle-nosed dolphins were seen near the Tappan Zee Bridge, and a "Florida" manatee swam up the East River. Harbor seals were sighted on Belmont Island and on Robbins Reef where they were common three hundred years ago; they've also been seen in Newark Bay, and in the Hudson near Hoboken, Yonkers, and Tarrytown, where they've bitten off the heads of shad caught in gill nets.

One day as Joe Shastay was motoring up the East River he saw a pair of fins coming toward his boat just north of the Williamsburg Bridge, a new sight for him after twelve years on the harbor. He shut his engine off and for five minutes watched two dark backs undulate toward the Upper Bay—harbor porpoises heading

164

Osprey fledglings in Jamaica Bay, near JFK International Airport. (Don Riepe, National Park Service)

downtown. Recently porpoises have even been seen in the Hudson as far north as Croton Point, some thirty-five miles from the Battery—the same waters where Peter Kalm watched them "play and tumble" some 250 years earlier.

The Hudson is one of the few North American or European rivers that still hosts spawning runs of all its native fishes. An Inwood building superintendent told me that he caught four sturgeon off the banks of Riverside Park; others also were catching them and letting them go under the impression they were sharks. A tag previously placed on one of them upriver by a fisheries biologist showed they were shortnose sturgeon, a federally endangered species that is flourishing in the Hudson River. And fewer tomcod struggle with cancer-ridden livers these days.

The swiftest of birds, the peregrine falcon, now nests and swoops from the Brooklyn, Verrazano Narrows, Throgs Neck,

Bayonne, Goethals, and George Washington Bridges—fourteen breeding pairs in total; friends have seen them chasing sanderlings along the surf's edge at Sandy Hook and Breezy Point. Bald eagles are seen migrating over Central Park and are becoming more numerous in the region—the first eaglet in a century hatched along the Hudson in 1997. Ospreys rear their young along Raritan Bay and in Jamaica Bay just one thousand yards from John F. Kennedy International Airport. Common terns have begun to nest on Hudson River piers near Tribeca. Hundreds of snow geese winter in Jamaica Bay after summering two thousand miles to the north in Hudson Bay; in cold weather snowy owls hunt along the Jersey City shore across from Liberty Island. A historic set of young soft-shell clams was found in Sandy Hook Bay and Raritan Bay that is producing hundreds of thousands of bushels of steamers. And Cathy Drew discovered young oysters clinging to the River Project pier.

New York Harbor took society's best shot and, without fanfare, bounced back up again. In the future, I for one will take pleasure when I dip my hands in its murky waters and look down the harbor's sweep to know that below, rivers of fish still flow through its depths, battalions of crabs clamber over its bottom, and a wondrous assortment of other creatures go bump in the night all day long.

Life in New York Harbor, stressed but resilient, overlooked but omnipresent, eternal yet surprising, goes on and on.

BIBLIOGRAPHY

Adams, Arthur G. *The Hudson: A Guidebook to the River.* New York: State University of New York Press, 1981. Mile-by-mile guide to major features and history of New York Harbor and the Hudson River.

Barlow, Elizabeth. *The Forests and Wetlands of New York City.* Boston: Little, Brown, 1969. Beguiling tour of New York City's wildest (natural) places.

Barnthouse, Lawrence W., Ronald J. Klauda, Douglas S. Vaughan, and Robert L. Kendall. *Science, Law, and Hudson River Power Plants.* Bethesda, Maryland: American Fisheries Society, 1988. Includes chapters on the physical Hudson River and its fishes.

Bean, Tarleton H. *Catalogue of the Fishes of New York State.* Albany: University of the State of New York, 1903. Anecdotal observations of harbor fishes from 1800s.

Beard, John. *Blue Water Views of Old New York, Including Long Island and the Jersey Shore.* Barre, Massachusetts: Scrimshaw, 1970. Good collection of images from old prints, with extracts from early writings on this reach of coastline.

Bone, Kevin (editor). *The New York Waterfront: Evolution and Building Culture of the Port and Harbor.* New York: Monacelli, 1997. Largely from public policy and architectural points of view; many excellent photographs.

Boyle, Robert H. *The Hudson River: A Natural and Unnatural History.* New York: W.W. Norton & Co., 1969. The bible on the Hudson's natural history and early conservation battles. Reprint in 1979 contains an epilogue for the years 1969–1978.

Brooks, William K. *The Oyster*. Baltimore: Johns Hopkins University Press, 1891. The classic work on oysters; Brooks foretold the collapse of the Chesapeake Bay oyster stock well before it occurred. Reprinted by same press in 1996.

Brydon, Norman F. *The Passaic River: Past, Present, Future*. New Brunswick, New Jersey: Rutgers University Press, 1974. Historical review of a major tributary of New York Harbor, including pollution and flooding problems.

Burger, Joanna (editor). *Before and After an Oil Spill: The Arthur Kill*. New Brunswick, New Jersey: Rutgers University Press, 1994. Detailed chronicle of New York Harbor's worst modern oil spill and its aftereffects, told from many viewpoints.

Burger, Joanna. *A Naturalist Along the Jersey Shore*. New Brunswick, New Jersey: Rutgers University Press, 1996. Mainly birds, including harbor herons.

Buttenweiser, Ann L. *Manhattan Water-Bound: Planning and Developing Manhattan's Waterfront from the Seventeenth Century to the Present*. New York: New York University Press, 1987. Evolution of Manhattan's shoreline, from colonial era to 1980s.

Cohen, Paul E., and Robert T. Augustyn. *Manhattan in Maps 1527–1995*. New York: Rizzoli, 1997. Lovely presentation across five centuries; includes history of each map.

Cronin, John, and Robert F. Kennedy, Jr. *The Riverkeepers*. New York: Scribner, 1997. Keeper movement and environmental regulation.

Danckaerts, Jasper. *Journal of Jasper Danckaerts 1679–1680*, edited by Bartlett Burleigh James and J. Franklin Jameson. New York: Scribner's, 1913. Dutchman's fascinating account of travels and life from Boston to Delaware in colonial times, with many observations of New York Harbor region.

Duffy, Francis J., and William H. Miller. *The New York Harbor Book*. Falmouth, Maine: TBW Books, 1986. General information on New York Harbor, with emphasis on shipping.

Frazier, Ian. "On Urban Shores." *The New Yorker*, January 10, 1994, pages 36–39. Metropolitan adventures with stripers.

Juet, Robert. *Juet's Journal: The Voyage of the* Half Moon *from 4 April to 7 November 1609*, edited by Robert M. Lunny. Newark: New Jersey Historical Society, 1959. Only firsthand account of Henry Hudson's voyage up the river.

Kalm, Peter. *Travels in North America*. Barre, Massachusetts: Imprint Society, 1972. Includes comments by Swedish naturalist on wildlife in New York Harbor region during mid-eighteenth century.

Kieran, John. *A Natural History of New York City*. Boston: Houghton Mifflin, 1959. Comprehensive guide by habitat type; mostly terrestrial, but some harbor coverage.

Kochiss, John M. *Oystering from New York to Boston*. Middletown, Connecticut: Wesleyan University Press, 1974. Oystering history and practices.

Limburg, Karin E., Mary Ann Moran, and William H. McDowell. *The Hudson River Ecosystem*. New York: Springer-Verlag, 1985. Fine scientific work, with chapters on PCBs and Westway.

Martin, Dudley B. "Shad in the Shadow of Skyscrapers." *National Geographic*, March 1947, pages 359–376. A look at the New Jersey shad fishery when it flourished.

Mayer, Garry F. (editor). *Ecological Stress and the New York Bight: Science and Management*. Columbia, South Carolina: Estuarine Research Federation, 1982. Scientific studies of the animals and environmental health of New York Harbor as its improvements were beginning to be seen.

McKenzie, Clyde L., Jr. *The Fisheries of Raritan Bay*. New Brunswick, New Jersey: Rutgers University Press, 1992. Thorough examination of these regionally important fisheries.

Metropolitan Sewerage Commission of New York. *Sewerage and Sewage Disposal in the Metropolitan District of New York and New Jersey*. New York: Martin P. Brown Press, 1910. Surprisingly sophisticated analysis of New York Harbor near its environmental nadir.

Mitchell, Joseph. *The Bottom of the Harbor*. Boston: Little, Brown, 1959. Classic writing on ambiance and characters of the harbor. The chapter in the book with the same title was originally published in *The New Yorker* in 1951.

Mittlebach, Margaret, and Michael Crewdson. *Wild New York: A Guide to the Wildlife, Wild Places, and Natural Phenomena of New York City*. New York: Crown, 1997. Wide-ranging survey.

New York City Department of Environmental Protection. *1997 New York Harbor Water Quality Survey*. New York, 1998. Useful summary of past and present (1997 was the 88th year of this annual survey) water quality conditions of the harbor.

New York–New Jersey Harbor Estuary Program. *Final Comprehensive Conservation and Management Plan.* New York, 1996. Government's management plans for the harbor.

Scott, Genio. *Fishing in American Waters.* New York: Harper & Brothers, 1869. Includes early accounts of several recreational fisheries around New York Harbor.

Seitz, Sharon, and Stuart Miller. *The Other Islands of New York City.* Woodstock, Vermont: Countryman Press, 1996. The harbor's islands: natural, manmade, and even lost.

Smith, C. Lavett. *The Inland Fishes of New York State.* Albany, New York: New York State Department of Environmental Conservation, 1985. Contains identification keys and information on many common New York Harbor fishes.

Squires, Donald F. *The Bight of the Big Apple.* New York Sea Grant Institute, 1981. Broad look at the New York Bight and New York Harbor.

Stanne, Stephen P., Roger G. Panetta, and Brian E. Forist. *The Hudson: An Illustrated Guide to the Living River.* New Brunswick, New Jersey: Rutgers University Press, 1996. Excellent contemporary crash course in the natural history and environment of the Hudson River.

Sullivan, Robert. *The Meadowlands: Wilderness Adventures at the Edge of a City.* New York: Scribner, 1998. Engaging romps through the swamps.

Weiss, Howard M. *Marine Animals of Southern New England and New York: Identification Keys to Common Nearshore and Shallow Water Macrofauna.* Connecticut: State Geological and Natural History Survey of Connecticut, 1995. Includes invertebrates, fishes, and birds that occur in New York Harbor.

Zeisel, William N., Jr. "Shark!!! and Other Sport Fish Once Abundant in New York Harbor." *Seaport,* Autumn 1990, pages 36–39. The shark presence in the nineteenth century.

Additional information on the environment of New York Harbor can be culled from the annual *Hudson River Almanac,* prepared by the New York State Department of Environmental Conservation and published by Purple Mountain Press; *Seaport* magazine, published by the South Street Seaport Museum; and *The Underwater Naturalist,* published by the American Littoral Society.

INDEX

Page numbers in **boldface** type refer to illustrations or photographs. Those in *italic* type refer to maps.

Able, Kenneth, 139–140, 142
Acid Grounds, chemical pollution and, 98
Acme Fertilizer Company, 107
Adler, Cyrus, 64
Advanced Identification Process (AVID), 139
Africa, cattle egrets and, 75
Agent Orange, 33
air pressure, waterways and, 27
albacore, false, 36
Albany, 36, 84
alewives, 36
algae, 91, 112, 151
Ali, Abu Moulta, 111
Alosa sapidissima (shad), 62
"Amboys" (oysters), 40
Ambrose, John Wolfe, 122
Ambrose Channel, 122
American eel, 62–65
American Heritage rivers, 158
American Museum of Natural History, 23, 35
American redstart warbler, 71
American shad, 36, 38
ammonia waste, 86
amphipods, 36, 124, 149
anchovies, 36, 104
anemones, ghost, rock walls and, 149
anglerfish, 37
anoxia, birds and, 68
Apalachicolas (Florida) oysters, 152
"Aquapatio" party barge, 125
"aquarium cars," 38
Army Corps of Engineers, 70, 105, 106, 111, 132–133, 137
arsenic (as contaminant), 82
Arthur Kill, 21, 26, 27, 49, 68, 69, 74, 75, 82, 86, 96–97, 100, 146, 147
Asian seaweed *(Codium fragile)*, 77
Astoria, Hell Gate and, 120
Atlantic City (New Jersey), garbage and, 98
Atlantic lobsters, 38

Atlantic Ocean, 29, 37, 62–63, 76, 77
Atlantic salmon, 37–38, 38
Atlantic sturgeon, 36, **136**
Atlantic tomcod, 92
Atlantic Twin, 133, 134
Audubon Society, New York City, 68, 69
AVID (Advanced Identification Process), 139
Avrin, David, 72
bacteria, 79, 162
baitfish, rock walls and, 148
bald eagles, Central Park and, 166
Baltimore (Maryland), bedrock and, 25
Barlow, Elizabeth *(The Forests and Wetlands of New York City)*, 145
barnacles, rock walls and, 148
Barnegat Bay, butterflyfish and, 35
Barnett Starch Works, 107
barn swallows, 140
Barren Island, 118
basking sharks, 37
bass. *See* specific types of bass
the Battery, 20, 26, 29, 34, 37, 49, 56, **100**, 142, 159-160, 165
Battery Park, 158, 159
Battery Park City, 116–117, 148
bay anchovies, electric-generating station and, 104
bay-breasted warbler, 71
Baykeeper Auxilliary, 126, 154
Bay of Fundy, striped bass and, 42
Bayonne Bridge, 97, 165
Bayonne Peninsula (New Jersey), chemical pollution and, 83
Bay Ridge, 109
Beacon, Hudson River and, 20
Beaver Street, 116
Bedloe's Island. *See* Liberty Island
bedrock, 25
Belford, commercial fishing and, 66
"Belford pirates," 66

Belmont Island, harbor seals and, 164
Benstock, Marcy, 140
benzene (as contaminant), 82
"biological oxygen demand," 84
birds, 22, 67-76, **73**, 97, 143, 149
Blackburnian warbler, 71
black-crowned night-herons, 68, 75
black drum, 37
blackpoll warbler, 71
Black Tom Channel, oysters and, 153
"blop-blops," 108
blowout tide, 28
bluebacks, 36
blue claw crabs, 32, 33, 36, 37, 62, 66, 73, 104, 149, 163
bluefish, 36, **47**, 48, 56, 91, 92-93, 98, 148
"bog people," 62
bonefish, 37
"boners" (of shad) and boning, 61–62
borers, marine, 93–96, **94**
borrow pits, 124
bottle-nosed dolphins, 164
Boyle, Robert H., 126
The Hudson River: A Natural and Unnatural History, 43
Bradley Beach (New Jersey), garbage and, 99
Bread and Cheese, 54
Breezy Point, 119, 121, 166
Bristol (Maine) oysters, 152
British soldier (lichen), 73
broad-billed sandpiper, 71–72
Broad Street, 116
the Bronx, 43–45, 86, 118
Brooklyn, 23, 86, 106, 109, 110, 118, 145, 158
Brooklyn Battery Tunnel, Westway project and, 131
Brooklyn Bridge, 149, 158, 165
Brooklyn Center for the Urban Environment, 109, 111
brook trout, 116
Brown, Adam, 42–43, 90
brown trout, 76
bryozoans, 103
Brzorad, John, 75–76
BT Nautilus, 97

buccaneers, 127
burrfish, 37
Bush, Irving T., 149
butterfish, 32
butterflyfish, 35
Buttermilk Channel, 109, 113
Butzel, Albert, 140, 142
cadmium (as contaminant), 112
Cahotateda (Native American term for Hudson River), 20
Camerons Line, 25
Canada geese, 74
Canada warbler, 71
Canadian Cove oysters, 152
canals, 117–118
Canal Street, 116
"Canal Street Plan," 41
Canarsee Indians, 109
Cape May (New Jersey), 21, 68, 77, 152
carbonic acid, 96
Carmer, Carl, 81
the Carolinas, oysters and, 50
CARP (Contamination and Assessment Reduction Project), 125
Carroll Street Bridge, 114
Carson, Rachel *(Silent Spring)*, 83
Carwitham Map, 40
catbird, 71
Category Three storm, 28
catfish, 26. *See also* marine catfish
Catskill, zebra mussels and, 77
Catskill Mountains, 20, 119
cattle egrets, 68, 75
Cedar Creek, 116
cedar waxwings, 127
Central America, birds and, 69, 74
Central Park, bald eagles and, 166
channel oysters, 153
"charismatic megafauna," 67
charter fishing, 46–47
chart series, DesBarres's Atlantic Neptune, 119
chemical pollution, 82. *See also* specific type of chemical
cherrystones, 49
Chesapeake Bay, 32, 42, 150, 151, 152
Chesapeake Biological Laboratory, 63
Chinatown, fishing education program and, 160
chlordane, fish and, 108
cholera, 112
Cholera Banks, 98
Cibro Savannah, 97

Citgo Petroleum Corporation, 97
City Island, oysters and, 42
City Parks Conservancy, 159
clams, 82, 124, 163, 166. *See also* southern marsh clam
Clason Point, sewage and, 86
Clean Air Campaign, 132, 143
Clean Water Act, 87
Clearwater, 159
Clermont, 116
climate, 27–30
Clinton, DeWitt, 38
Coast Guard, 22, 28
cobia, 37
Coch, Nicholas, 28
Codium fragile (Asian seaweed), 77
Collect Pond, 116
College Point, 49
Columbia University, 145
combined sewer overflows (CSOs), 90
commercial fishing, 58, 65, 66, 67, 73
condoms (Coney Island whitefish), 50
Coney Island, 29, 30, 54, 86, **101**, 116, 162
Coney Island Arctic Ice Bears, 30
Coney Island whitefish (condoms), 50
Connecticut, 20, 92
Consolidated Edison, 103–104, 110, 158
contamination. *See* pollution
Contamination and Assessment Reduction Project (CARP), 125
copper (as contaminant), 82
coral reefs, 35, 145
Coriolis force, 26
Corlears Hook, 144
cormorants, double-crested, 72–73, **73**
cornetfish, 37
Cotuit (Massachusetts) oysters, 152
cove oysters, 152
crabbing, 62, 65, 73. *See also* specific types of crabs
crabs. *See* crabbing; specific types of crabs
Crassotrea virginica, 151–152
creeks, oysters and, **40**
croakers, 32
Cross Bay Boulevard Bridge, oysters and, 49
Croton-on-Hudson, oysters and, 39

Croton Point, harbor porpoises and, 165
Croton River, sewage and, 84
CSOs (combined sewer overflows), 90, 148
ctenophores, 104
cunners, 35, 148, 154
Cuomo, Mario, 132, 137
Cuttyhunk (Massachusetts) oysters, 152
damselflies, spartina and, 146
Danckaerts, Jasper, 34, 65, 93, 109, 119
DDT, 72, 83
"Dead Sea," 89
Degraw and Hoyt Streets, 113
Delaware Bay, horseshoe crabs and, 74
Delaware River, keepers and, 126
depth of water, 118–119
DesBarres's Atlantic Neptune chart series, 119
detritus, electric-generating stations and, 103
development, water. *See* waterfront development
Development Commission (New Jersey), 131
Dew, C. Braxton, 148
diabase, 25
diadromous fish, 63
diamondback terrapins, 128
Diamond Shamrock Company, 33
dieldrin, fish and, 108
diking, 128
dioxins, 33, 82, 163
ditching, 128
"dock rats" (petty thieves), 86
dolphins, bottle-nosed, 164
double-crested cormorants, 72–73, **73**
Dreamland, 54
dredging, 118, 119, 120, 122–125
Drew, Cathy, 34–35, 77, 166
Driftmaster, 105
driftwood, 98–99, **100**
drums. *See* black drum; red drum
ducks, 116, 146
Duffy-Anderson, Janet, 140, 141
Dutch colonists, spartina and, 145
dying-fish phenomenon, 92–93
E and F subway lines, 118
East Channel, 121
East Fourteenth Street, garbage and, 103

172

East High Meadow Island, 22
East Ninety-sixth Street, pollution and, 82
East River, 20, **20**, 21-22, 26, 28, 29, 41, 42, 43-45, **47**, 49, 50, 51, 55, 68, **73**, 90, 93, 95, 103, 107, 137, 144, 148, 158, 159, 164-65
ecology, 29–30
"eel grip," 64
eels, 62–65, 66, 108, 149
egrets, 68, 72
Eighth Avenue, garbage and, 97
electric-generating stations, Consolidated Edison, 103–104, 110
Elizabeth (New Jersey), 68–69, 124
Elizabeth River, 27
Ellis Island, 36, 48, 76, 116
elvers, 63
England, landfills and, 102
Environmental Defense Fund, 142
Environmental Protection Agency, 132, 139
environmental stress, birds and, 75–76
Erie Basin, 67
Erie Canal, 110
estuaries, 19–21, 26, 35–36. *See also* Estuary of National Significance; Harbor Estuary Program; New York/New Jersey Harbor Estuary
Estuary of National Significance, 46
Europe, zebra mussels and, 77–78
European perwinkle, 77
European settlers (or colonists), 22, 39, 66, 127
eutrophication, 91
Exxon, 96–97, 146, 147, 158
false albacore, 36
fauna or flora, 29, 34, 76–79, 102
FDR Drive, 95, 103
fecal coliform bacteria, 162
Federal Drug Administration, 108
Federal Oil Pollution Act of 1924, 83
fertilizer *(munnawhatteaug)*, 62. *See also under* sludge
fiddler crabs, 75, 131, 146
Fifteenth Ward Smelling Committee, 107
Fifty-ninth Street, Westway project and, 142

Fifty-ninth Street Bridge, striped bass and, 43
finfish, toxics survey and, 162–163
Fink, Bill, 159
fin rot, 91
fish, 26–27, 31–39, 45-46, 48, 49, 56, 61, 65, 66, 75, 79, 84, 91–93, 104, 105, 108, 129, 132, 134, 139, **141**, 142, 148, 149, 151, 161–163, 165
fishing, 47, 50, 51, 55-62, **59**, 60, 66–67, 105, 159–160
Fishkill Creek, salmon and, 38
Fishport, 67
the "flagman," 135–136
floatables, 102
Floaters' Week, 134
Floating the Apple, 159
flooding, 27–28
Flood Rock explosion, **120**
flora, 76, 102
Florida, 126, 152
Florida manatee, East River and, 164
flounder, winter, **141**, 142, 148, 162–163
Floyd Bennett Field, 118
fluke bait, 129
flukes, 36, 49, 91
Flushing Bay, 21, 55, 124
Flushing Meadow Park, Hudson River and, 23
flying gurnard, 37
Fordham schist, 25
forest, 102, 127–128
The Forests and Wetlands of New York City (Barlow), 145
Fort Lafayette, 118
Fort Lee (New Jersey), fishing and, 58, **59**
Fort Wadsworth, sewage and, 86
Fort Washington, oysters and, 153
Fort Washington Heights, 116
Fort Washington Park, 158
Forty-second Street, 116, 131
Forty-seventh Street, climate and, 29
foureyes, 35
Frazier, Ian, 42
Freeke's Mill, 110
Fresh Kills, 74, 100–102, 147
Friends of Fishes, 159–160
Friends of Gateway, 158
Friends of Gerritsen Creek, 158
Friends of Harlem on the River, 159
Friends of the Rockaways, 158
Frying Pan, 54

Fulton, Robert, 116
Fulton Fish Market, 66, 67
fungi, 95
furans, 163
Gabriel, Steve, 43–45
gamefishing, 46
garbage, 81, 97–104, **98, 99, 100, 101, 104,** 116, 117, 125, 134–135, 152
Gateway National Seashore, habitats and, 29
geese, spartina and, 146. *See also* Canada geese; snow geese
General Electric, 82, 161
geography, 19–22
George Washington Bridge, 28, 60, 63, 165
ghost anemones, rock walls and, 148
Giuliani, Rudolph, 93
gizzard shad, 32
glaciers. *See* Ice Age
Gloria Michelle, 31
glossy ibis, 68, 74, 75
gneiss, 25
Goethals Bridge, 146, 165
government, 55–58, 66–67, 85–86, 143. *See also* specific names of agencies, authorities, departments, etc.
Governors Island, 22, 109
Gowane's Creek (Gowanus Creek), 109
Gowanus Canal, 21, 106, 108–114, 111–112, **112,** 113, 155, 163
Gowanus Creek, 109
Gowanus Expressway, 111
"Gowanus" oysters, 109
Grain Terminal, 110
Grand Central Parkway, 23
Grand Central Station, Oyster Bar and, 152
grass shrimp, 36, 154
the Graught, 116
great egrets, 68, 75
Great Hurricane of 1938, 28
Great Kills, garbage and, 102
Great Lakes, 110
Great South Bay, oysters and, 152
green crabs, 77
green herons, 68
Greenpoint, 95, 108
gribbles *(Limnoria),* 95
Griesa, Thomas, 132, 137
Griffis, Bud, 137
groupers, 35
Guggenheim Museum, 140
Gulf of Mexico, southern marsh clam and, 77

Gulf Stream, 35, 63
gulls, 27, 74
Habitat Committee, 139
habitats, 125, 138–155, 158, 161
"habitat science," 143
Hackensack Meadowlands (New Jersey), 25, 125–131, **129**
Hackensack Meadowlands Development Commission, 128, 129, 146–147
Hackensack River, 20–21, 29, 33, 124, 125–131, 148
hake, 32, 37
Halfmoon, 37, 38, 119
Hallett's Reef, 111
Hamptons, striped bass and, 42
Harbor Estuary Program, 46, 148
Harbor Festival, 158
harbor herons, 69, 72, 75–76, 97
Harbor Herons Program, 69
harbor porpoises, 164–165
harbor seals, 164
Harbor Survey Program, 87
Harlem, 160
Harlem River, 37, 51, 117–118, 145, 158, 159
Harlem River Expressway, salt marsh and, 145
Harlem Ship Canal, 118
Harmon Cove (New Jersey), 130
Harper's Weekly, 107
HARS (Historic Area Remediation Site), 124
Hart Island, 22
Hartz Mountain Corporation, 128, 129
hawks, red-tailed, Passaic River and, 106
Heel Tap, 54
Hell Gate, 51–55, **52–53**, 66, **120**, 120–121, **121**
Hen and Chicken, 54
hepatitis, 112
hermit crabs, rock walls and, 149
herons, 74–75. *See also* harbor herons; specific types of herons
herring, 36, 37, 62
herring gulls, 74
Highlands-to-Ocean Fund (H$_2$O Fund), 158
Historic Area Remediation Site (HARS), 124
history of Harbor, 19–30
Hoboken, harbor seals and, 164
Hoffman Island, 118

Hog Island, Great Hurricane of 1938 and, 28
Hogs Back, 54
Holland-America, 140
Holland Tunnel, sediment and, 25
Horenstein, Sidney, 23
horseshoe crabs, 33, 73–74
horse urine, piers and, 95
house wren, 71
Howland Hook, 122
H$_2$O Fund (Highlands-to-Ocean Fund), 158
Hudson, Henry, 37, 39, 63, 83, 115
Hudson Bay, snow geese and, 166
Hudson Canyon, Ice Age and, 23
Hudson River, 19-21, **20**, 23, 25-28, **28**, 29, 35, 36, 37-38, 41, 46, 48, 50, 62, 64-65, 77-79, 84, 91-93, 108, 116, 122-123, 126, 131-132, 133, 137, 139, 142, 154, 158, 159, 160-161, 162, 164, 165, 166
The Hudson River: A Natural and Unnatural History (Boyle), 43
Hudson River Almanac, 34
Hudson River Foundation, 108, 139
Hudson Riverkeeper, 126
Hudson River Park Alliance, 142
Hudson River Swimmers, 162
Hudson Valley, 20, 27, 91, 125
human waste. *See* sewage
hurricanes, 28
Hussar, 51
ibis, glossy, 68, 74, 75
Ice Age (Pleistocene Age), 22–23
ichtyofauna, 35
illegal fishing. *See* poaching
Indians (Native Americans), 20, 23, 39, 62, 109, 130
industrial park, 149
Ingold, Ron, 59–62
Ingold, Scott, 61, 63
Inwood, 144–145, 165
Inwood Heights Park Alliance, 145
Inwood marble, 25
Isbrandtsen shipping line, 110
islands of the Harbor, 21–22
Isle of Meadows, 72, 74
Jamaica Bay, 21, 23, 26, 28, 29, 42, 49, 57, 58, 65, 74, 118, 124, 163, **165**, 166

Jamaica Bay Wildlife Refuge, 71–72
"Jamaicas" (oysters), 40
Japanese shore crabs, 77
Jefferies Hook Lighthouse, 63
Jersey City (New Jersey), **85,** 117, 134, 153, 166
Jersey City Heights (New Jersey), 126
JFK International Airport, 118, **165,** 166
"jimmies" (male blue claw crabs), 33
Juet, Robert, 37, 83
Just, Anthony, 129
Kalm, Peter, 40, 66, 161, 165
Kearny, sediment and, 124
keepers, 126–127
Kenny's Killer Killifish, 129
Kerlinger, Paul, 68–74
Keyport (New Jersey), oysters and, **40**
Kieran, John (*A Natural History of New York City*), 164
killifish, 35, 65, 129–130, 146
Kill Van Kull, 21, 58, 65, 69, 86, 96–97, **104,** 105
Kirchner, Karl, 65
Klein, Robert, 50
Klondike Banks, 98
Koch, Edward, 45, 137
lady crabs, rock walls and, 149
ladyfish, 37
Lafayette, Marquis de, 32
Lafayette Island, 118
lafayettes, 32
La Guardia Airport, striped bass and, 55
Lake, Tom, 34, 159–160
Lake Erie, zebra mussels and, 77, 79
Lake Flushing, Wisconsin glacier and, 25
Lake Hackensack, Wisconsin glacier and, 25
Lake Passaic, Wisconsin glacier and, 25
Lake Tear of the Clouds, Hudson River and, 20
landfills, 99–101, 102, 118, 132, 137, 148
laughing gulls, 74
"Lavender Lake" (Gowanus Canal), 110
lead (as contaminant), 82, 112
Lehigh Valley (Pennsylvania), 117
Liberty Island, 40, 48, 153
Liberty State Park, oysters and, 153
lichen, 73

light, **141,** 142, 151
lime, oysters and, 41
Limnoria (gribbles), piers and, 95
limpets, slipper, 155
Lincoln Tunnel, sediment and, 25
Lispenard Meadows, 116
Little Hell Gate, 116
Little Oyster Islands, 40
Little Red Lighthouse, 63
The Little Red Lighthouse and the Great Gray Bridge (Swift and Ward), 63
liver cancer, in fish, 92
lobsters or lobstering, 38, 65, 66
Long Beach, 28, 99
Long Island, 23, 28, 29, 66, 98, 99, 152
Long Island Railroad, 118
Long Island Sound, 20, 21, 26, 27, 42, 84, 120, 126, 133
Longstreth, Ben, 154–155, 163
Lower New York Bay (Lower Bay), 19, 21, 23, 36, 66, 97, 119
lumpfish, 37
Maass, Rob, 108, 113
Maccarone, Alan, 75–76
mackerel, Spanish, 36
MacNeill Park, oysters and, 49
Maine, Bristol oysters and, 152
manatee, Florida, East River and, 164
Manhattan, 20, **20,** 25, 26, 28, 34, 36, 37, 40-41, **41,** 47, 48, 50, 58-59, 64, 65, 81–82, 84, 86, 87–88 99, 106, 116, 118, 134–135, 144-145
Manhattan Criminal Court, 116
mantis shrimp, 33
map of New York Harbor, *24*
Marble Hill, 118
marine borers, 93–96, **94**
marine catfish, 37
Marine Enforcement Unit (New York State Department of Environmental Conservation), 57
Markowski, Ed, 67
marsh hawk, 74
marsh snails, 75
Martha's Vineyard (Massachusetts), striped bass and, 43, 45
Maspeth Heights, 106
Maspeth Marsh, 106
Massachusetts, 20, 152
Matsil, Marc, 102, 146

Meadowlands (New Jersey). *See* Hackensack Meadowlands
medical wastes, 102
menhaden ("mossbunkers"), 32, 62, 65, 92–93
mercury (as contaminant), 82, 112
methane gas, 86, 89, 101, 108
Metropolitan Sewerage Commission of New York, 81, 86, 99, 153
Metropolitan Sewerage Commission Report, 153
Metzger, Charles, 140
Midland Beach, swimming and, 162
Mill Basin, oysters and, 49
Miller, Kiah, 87–88
Mills Corporation (Virginia), 131
Minetta Brook, 116
minnows, 111, 129
Mitchell, Joseph, 112
Mohawk River Valley, Hudson River and, 20
mollusk, type of *(Teredo),* 95
Montauk, Lower New York Bay (Lower Bay) and, 21
Montayne's Rivulet, 116
moon phases, 26, 28, 74
moraines, 22–23
Morris Canal, 117, **117**
Moses, Robert, 118
mosquitoes, 144
"mossbunkers" (menhaden), 32, 62, 65, 92–93
Mott, Peter, 68
Mott Basin, fishing and, 57
Mount Marcy, Hudson River and, 20
Mount Spike, 124
mud crabs, 77, 154
"Mud Dump," 123, 124
Muhheakunnuk (Native American term for Hudson River), 20
Muir, John, 109
Municipal Art Society, 142
munnawhatteaug (Indian term for fertilizer), 62
muskrats, 65–66
mussels, 77–79, 146
Myers, Keith, 55
National Alliance of River, Sound, and Baykeepers, 126
National Geographic, 58
Native Americans (Indians), 20, 23, 39, 62, 109, 130
A Natural History of New York City (Kieran), 164

Natural Resources Defense Council, 142
Natural Resources Group, 102, 146, 147
Navesink River, Lower New York Bay (Lower Bay) and, 21
"nearshore containment areas," 124
Negro Head, 54
neotropical migratory songbirds ("neotrops"), 69–70, 71
Newark (New Jersey), 106, 158
Newark Bay, 21, 31-32, 33, 69, 82, 118, 124, 163, 164
Newburgh, Hudson River and, 20
New England, 23, 66, 76
New Jersey, 26, 28, 40, 58, 60, 73, 83, 124, 129-130, 131, 139
New Jersey Department of Environmental Protection, 45–46, 67
New Jersey Marine Sciences Corporation, 133
New Jersey Turnpike, swallow nests and, 128
New Settlement Apartments, 159
Newtown Creek, 21, 51, 106–108, 143
New York (state), 23, 26, 40, 56, 73, 74, 91
New York Bay Pollution Commission, 86
New York Bight, 21, 27, 29, 66, 67, 91, 97-98, 123
New York City, 22, 28, 37, 51, 55, 67, 68, 82, 84, 86, 87, 90, 100, 162
New York City Audubon Society, 68, 69
New York City Department of Parks, 102, 147
New York City Department of Transportation, 96
New York City Harbor Survey, 162
New York City Outward Bound Center, 159
New York City Rare Bird Alert, 71
New York/New Jersey Harbor Baykeeper, 126
New York/New Jersey Harbor Estuary Program, 46, 139, 158
New York State Department of Environmental Conservation, 45, 57

New York State Department of Transportation, 132
New York State Health Department, 93
New York Times, 55, 106, 114
New York Yankees, 93
Nichols Chemical Works, 107
night-herons, 68, 140
1998 International Coastal Cleanup, 158
Ninth Street and Avenue C, wetlands and, 144
Ninth Street Bridge, 113
nitrogen, 91, 150
nor'easters, 27
North America, 22, 25, 38, 63, 69, 75, 76, 77-78
North Brother Island, 22
the Northeast, striped bass and, 42
North River Sewage Treatment Facility, 87-90, 137
nor'westers, 28
Nova Scotia, European periwinkle and, 77
Ocean Grille, oysters and, 152
oil or oil spills, 83, 96-97, 98, 107-108, 112, 147
Old Place Creek Marsh, 146
Old Wreck Brook, 116
125th Street, striped bass and, 43
137th and 145th Streets, pilings and, 137
Operation Sail, 158
Orvis, 116
osmosis, 146
ospreys, **165,** 166
Overpeck Creek (New Jersey), 128
owls, snowy, Jersey City (New Jersey) and, 166
oxygen deficiency, 68, 78-79, 84, 86, 87, 91, 92-93, 108, 112, 162
Oyster Bar, 152
Oyster Bay, oysters and, 152
oystercatchers, **69**
Oyster Island, 40
"oyster rows," 41
oysters, 39-42, 37, **39, 40,** 82, 109, 149-155, 163
oyster toadfish, 154-155
the Pacific, fish and shellfish and, 38
Pacific chinook salmon, 38
Pacific salmon, 63
PAHs (polynuclear aromatic hydrocarbons), 82, 92
the Palisades, 25, 130

Palisades Mountains, Ice Age and, 23
Paramour Island (Virginia) oysters, 152
Parks Council, 142
Parsons, Brinckeroff & Quade, 132
Passaic River, 20-21, 27, 33, 105-106, 106, 158
Passaic River Coalition, 106
Pastime Princess, 160
Paterson (New Jersey), Ice Age and, 23
Paterson Plank Road, 127
PCBs (polychlorinated biphenyls), 61, 82, 93, 108, 161
peacock bass, 76
Pearl Street, oyster shells and, 41-42
Peconic Bay, oysters and, 152
Peekskill, 27, 78, 133
Pennsylvania, sediment and, 124
Penobscot River (Maine), 38
peregrine falcons, 165-166
periwinkle, European, 77
pesticide. *See* DDT
petroleum. *See* oil or oil spills
Philadelphia, bedrock and, 25
photosynthesis, Hudson River and, 78
phytoplankton, Hudson River and, 78-79
Pier 26, 34, 35, 77, 162
Pier 32, 162
Pier 40, 140-142, **141**
Pier 76, 123
piers, 93-95, **94,** 117, 134, 138-143, 149, 166
pilings, 137-143, 153
pinhookers, 56
pipefish, 35, 149
piping plover, 147
plants. *See* flora
Pleistocene Age (Ice Age), 22-23
poaching, 56, 57, 58, 66-67
"pocket marshes," 148
pollution, 32, 33, 37, 42, 46, 57, 61, 65, 68, 75-76, 83, 86, 91-95, **94,** 105-114, 122, 124-131, 138, 153, 155, 159. 162-163
polyaromatic hydrocarbons, 162-163
polychlorinated biphenyls (PCBs), 61
polynuclear aromatic hydrocarbons (PAHs), 82
porgies, 32, 49

porpoises, harbor, 164-165
Port Authority, 67, 110, 122
Port Elizabeth, 122
Portland (Maine), herring gulls and, 74
Port Liberté (New Jersey), chemical pollution and, 83
Port Newark, 105, 122
the Pot, 54
Poughkeepsie, 19, 38
prairie warbler, 71
Pralls Island, 72, 73-74
Prince Bay, oystering and, **39**
Prince Edward Island, Canadian Cove oysters and, 152
Queens, 23, 86, 106, 118, 120, 145
Queens College, 28
radionuclide studies, 123
Rahway River, 27
rail system, fish and, 38
rainwater, Fresh Kills landfill and, 102
Randalls Island, 116
Rangia (southern marsh clam), 77
Raritan Bay, 39, 42, 66, 162, 166
Raritan River, 21, 23, 38
rats, 103, 106
Ratzer Map, 144
Reagan economic boom, 45
recognition views, 119
red drum, 37
red hake, 37
Red Hook, 109, 113, 158
red knots, 74
redstart warbler, 71
red-tailed hawks, Passaic River and, 106
Reefkeeper, 126
reefs, Hell Gate and, 51-54, **52-53,** 120, **120.** *See also under* oysters
Rhode Island, birds and, 68
Rikers Island, 22, 116
Rivera, Geraldo, son of, 61
River and Harbor Act of 1888, 117
river herring, 36
River Project, 34-35, 154, 166
Riverside Park, 158, 165
Robbins Reef, 27, 58, 164
Robert H. Boyle, 128, 130
Rockaway Beach, Great Hurricane of 1938 and, 28
Rockaway Inlet, Lower New York Bay (Lower Bay) and, 21
Rockaways, shellfish and, 162

"Rockaways" (oysters), 40
rock crabs, rock walls and, 149
Rockefeller, John D., 107
Rockefeller Brothers Fund, 158
rock-faced walls, 148
Rocking the Boat Program, 159
rodents, 116
Roosevelt Island, 21
ruby-crowned kinglet, 81
rudderfish, tropical banded, 49
ruddy turnstones, 74
Rutgers University, 139
"Sailing Up, Sailing Down,"
    160
St. Mary's City (Maryland),
    oysters and, 152
salm and *salmpie* (Dutch terms
    for salmon or trout), 38
salmon, 37–38, 63
Salmo salar, 38
salt hay *(Spartina patens)*, 145
salt marshes, 25, 144–148
sand-builder worms, rock walls
    and, 149
sanderlings, 74, 166
sandpiper, broad-billed, 71–72
sand shrimp, 36, 149
Sandy Hook, 29, 39, 119, 120,
    121–122, 123, 166
Sandy Hook Bay, clams and,
    166
Sandy Hook Channel, water
    depth and, 119
San Francisco, 76
San Francisco Bay, keepers and,
    126
Sargasso Sea, eels and, 63
sawdust, salmon and, 37
Saw Mill Creek Preserve, **147**
Sawmill Marsh (New Jersey),
    130–131
Schutters Island (Dutch term
    for Shooters Island), 70
scouring, 123
Scribner's Monthly, 95
sculpins, 32
sea bass, 35, 154
seabirds, Sunset Park
    Restoration and, 149
Seagate Beach, swimming and,
    162
Seagull Grounds, garbage and,
    97–98
seagulls, 27, 74, 97–98
sea herring, 37
sea horses, 35
sea level, 26
seals, harbor, 164
sea robins, 32, 49
seasons, 26, 29–30, 36–37, 39,
    40, 48

sea squirts, 77, 154
sea trout, 39
sea turtles, 164
seaweed, Asian *(Codium fragile)*,
    77
Secaucus (New Jersey), 125,
    129, 130
Secor, David, 63–64
sediment, 25, 33, 122–124, 130,
    148, 153
1777 Plan of Hell Gate, 54
sewage, 27, 43, 81–91, **82, 83,**
    85, 87–90, 112, 127, 153, 162
shad, 32, 36, 38, 58–59, **59,**
    60–61, 62, 63, 66, 105, 164
sharks, 37, **50,** 50–51, 111–112,
    112
Shastay, Joe, 46–49, **47,** 56,
    164–165
Sheehan, Bill, 125–130
sheepshead, 37
Sheepshead Bay, fish and, 37
shellfish, 57, 65, 66, 92, 105,
    149, 151, 162-163
Sherman, Ben, 55
Sherman Creek, **144,** 145
"shifting baselines," 161
ships, 118–120, 122
shipworm *(Teredo navalis)*, 77
Shooters Island, 22, 70, 143
shorebirds, 74, 147
Shorewalkers, 64
shortnose sturgeon, Riverside
    Park and, 165
Shrewsbury River, Lower New
    York Bay (Lower Bay) and,
    21
shrimp, 33, 36, 75, 149, 151,
    154
Sierra Club, 132, 143
Silent Spring (Carson), 83
siltation, 42, 123
silver hake, 37
silver perch, 32
silverside minnows, Gowanus
    Canal and, 111
Sixtieth Street, fishing and, 58
"sleek," 98
slipper limpets, 155
sludge, 86–90, 106–107, 108,
    112, 153
Smerz, Artie, 43–45
Smith, C. Lavett, 35
Smith, M.W., Jr., 132
Smith Point, garbage and, 98
snails, marsh, 75
Snake Hill (New Jersey), **129,**
    130
snakes, Snake Hill (New Jersey)
    and, 130
snapper bluefish, 32, 148

snappers, 35
snow geese, 166
snowy egrets, 68, 74, 75
snowy owls, Jersey City (New
    Jersey) and, 166
songbirds, neotropical migrato-
    ry, 69–70
"sooks" (female blue claw
    crabs), 33
Soundview Park, 118
South America, 69, 74, 75
South Beach, swimming and,
    162
South Brother Island, 22,
    72–73, **73**
southern marsh clam *(Rangia)*,
    77
Spanish mackerel, 36
Sparkill, Ice Age and, 23
spartina, 145–146
Spartina alterniflora, 145–146
Spartina patens, 145
spat (young oysters), 154, 155
spotfin butterflyfish, 35
Spuyten Duyvil, 63, 135, 148
St. Lawrence River, zebra mus-
    sels and, 79
Standard Oil, 107
Staten Island, 23, 29, 37, 66,
    86, 93, 101, 102, 118, 119,
    122, 146, **147, 150,** 158, 162
Staten Island Ferry, 48
Statue of Liberty, hurricanes
    and, 28
steamboats, salmon and, 37
Stewart, Lance, 148
storms, 27, 28
streams (sewer outfalls), 27
striped bass, 32, 36, 38, 42–45,
    44, 47, 48, 54–57, 60–61, 63,
    91, 93, 136, 137, 142, 148,
    160, 163
sturgeon, 36, 105, 135, **136,** 165
Stuyvesant Cove, parks and, 158
Stuyvesant Town, salt marshes
    and, 148
Subway Grounds, garbage and,
    97
sulfuric acid-acid sulfate wastes,
    98
Sunken Meadow Island, 116
Sunset Park Restoration, 149
Superfund, Newark (New
    Jersey) and, 106
Suszkowski, Dennis, 108
swadelen (Dutch term for type
    of storm), 28
swallow nests, New jersey
    Turnpike and, 128
Swift, Hildegarde H., and
    Lynde Ward *(The Little Red*

Lighthouse and the Great Gray Bridge), 63
Swinburne Island, 118
Tallman Island, 118
Tappan Zee Bridge, 59, 164
Tarrytown, harbor seals and, 164
tautogs, 35, 38, 58, 142, 148
Tea-water Spring, 116
Teredo (type of mollusk), piers and, 95, 96
Teredo navalis (shipworm), 77
Teredo worms, 103
terns, 166
terrapins, Saw Mill Marsh (New Jersey) and, 131
Throgs Neck Bridge, peregrine falcons and, 165
tides, 25–27, 28, 47, 60, 74, 102–103, 119
Tiffany Street Pier, 96
timbering, 127–128
Tin Can Grounds, garbage and, 97
toadfish, oyster, 154–155
toluene (as contaminant), 82
tomcod, 32, 92, 142, 165
topography of Harbor, 22
tornado, waterborne, 27
toxics survey, 162–163
trash. *See* garbage
Tribeca, terns and, 166
tropical banded rudderfish, 49
trout, 38–39, 76, 116
Troy (New York), 19–20, 38
Trust for Public Land, 142
tuna, 36
tunicates ("sea grapes"), 103, 148
Turtle Bay, climate and, 29
turtles, Hackensack River and, 128
Twentieth Street, salt marshes and, 148
Twenty-third Street, Coney Island Arctic Ice Bears and, 30
typhoid fever, 42, 82, 112. *See also* Typhoid Mary
Typhoid Mary, 22
Union (New Jersey), 126
United Kingdom, fauna and, 77
United Nations, **44,** 49, 73
United States, 42, 75
U.S. & Canada Degreasing Syndicate, 107
U.S. Congress, 121, 122, 132
U.S. Environmental Protection Agency, 45
U.S. Fish and Wildlife Service, 132

U.S. National Marine Fisheries Service, 31, 132
Upper New York Bay (Upper Bay), 19, 21, 22, 23, 27, 28, 29, 40, 48, 65, 87, 98, 159, 164
Upper West Side, striped bass and, 42
urine, piers and, horse, 95
U Thant Island, 48, 73, 116
Van Wyck Expressway, 23
vegetation, Sunset Park Restoration and, 149
Vermont, Hudson River and, 20
Verrazano, Giovanni da, 115–116
Verrazano Bridge, Sunset Park Restoration and, 149
Verrazano Narrows, 20, 23, 26, 51, 58, 164
Verrazano Narrows Bridge, 36, 65, 118, 165
Vesey Street, sharks and, 51
Virginia, Paramour Island oysters and, 152
wading birds, 67–76, 149
walls, rock-faced, 148
Wall Street crash of 1987, 138
warblers, 71, 74
Ward, Lynde, and Hildegarde H. Swift *(The Little Red Lighthouse and the Great Gray Bridge)*, 63
Wards Island, 116
Washington, D.C., bedrock and, 25
Washington Square, 116
waste, human. *See* sewage
waste matters. *See* chemical pollution; garbage; pollution; sewage
Watchung Mountains, Ice Age and, 23
waterborne tornado, 27
water depth, 118–119
waterfowl, Sunset Park Restoration and, 149
waterfront access, fishing and, 56
waterfront development, 45–46, 106, 130, 131–143, 157
water quality, New York City Outward Bound Center and, 159
water rats, 106
Waterside, pilings and, 137
waterspout, 27
Water Street, 117
water-treatment (or water-quality) programs, 87, 102

weakfish, 32, 39, 47, 91
weather, 27–28
West Side Highway (Westway). *See* Westway (West Side Highway)
Westway (West Side Highway), 131–143, **135,** 148–149
Westway Study, **135**
wetlands, 143–144
whale, Kill Van Kull and, **104,** 105
whelks, rock walls and, 149
"Whitehalls," 159
Whitehall Street, 51
White Mountain gneiss, 25
Williamsburg Bridge, harbor porpoises and, 164
Willner, Andy, 126–127
winter flounder, 141, 142, 148, 162–163
Wisconsin glacier, 23, 25
Wolley, Reverend Charles, 27
World War I, 83, 110
World War II, 66
worms, 65, 77, 103, 124, 149, 151
yellow-crowned night-herons, 68, 75
yellow fever, 118
Yellow Hook (Bay Ridge), 109
Yellow Mills, 110
yellow warbler, 71
Yonkers, 87, 136, 164
Yorkville, 43
zebra mussels, 77–79
Zeisel, William, 38, 50–51

178